Praise for *Royal Coachman*

"The sport, like this book, is not about engineering but about beauty and other things we weren't meant to ever fully understand."

—Geoffrey Norman, *American Way*

"Schullery writes of his fellow human beings with a sense of redemption, persistent good will, and humor."

—Daniel Zantzinger, *Daily Camera* (Boulder, CO)

"This is the kind of book that fly-fishing enthusiasts will embrace, and which itself will embrace the casual fisherman."

—Dan Danborn, *Arvada Community News* (Denver, CO)

"While I would always rather be on the water, *Royal Coachman* makes for fine reading when we can't be out there casting for trout."

—*Michigan Out-of-Doors*

"Paul Schullery captures the pleasures of fishing better than most in *Royal Coachman*."

—*Republican-American* (Waterbury, CT)

"In *Royal Coachman* Paul Schullery is at once an erudite emissary of the angle and consummate trout bum. And because not everyone can be both, we praise him as an American original."

—James Prosek, author of *Joe and Me: An Education in Fishing and Friendship* and *Trout: An Illustrated History*

"Few have as much passion for fly-fishing as Paul Schullery, and even fewer have his endless curiosity about the history of the sport, but it is his awesome talent as a writer that makes *Royal Coachman* such fine and fun reading. He makes his passion and his knowledge so compelling that they become yours as much as his."

—Gary LaFontaine, author of *Dry Fly: New Angles*

"Paul Schullery's prose flows smoothly and clearly as a trout-filled spring creek. His knowledge of fly-fishing history and his insights into its social currents are without peer. *Royal Coachman* is a rich, enjoyable, honest, provocative, and thoroughly entertaining book."

—Steve Raymond,
author of *Rivers of the Heart: A Fly-Fishing Memoir*

"For decades, Paul Schullery has been an astute and entertaining contributor to the literature of fly-fishing. He knows the fascinating history of fly-fishing better than any working writer. And he has fished his arm off in American waters. He is also a first-class naturalist. He gathers all his talents in *Royal Coachman*, by far the best of recent personal fly-fishing narratives."

—Christopher Camuto, author of *A Fly Fisherman's Blue Ridge*
and *Another Country: Journeying
Toward the Cherokee Mountains*

"Paul Schullery has followed angling history with rod and flies for much of his life, living among the better trout streams and finding none he didn't like. A student of fly-fishing will appreciate his solid information and then realize it never seemed so entertaining before. And despite his wry accounts of angling fumbles, it is impossible to read *Royal Coachman* without realizing that the author is a master fly-fisherman who has earned his reputation."

—Charles F. Waterman, author of
History of American Angling and *Fishing in America*

"Having depended on Paul Schullery for so much of my reporting about fish and wildlife issues in and around Yellowstone, I picked up this book with enormous expectations. I was not disappointed. I gulped it at one sitting, with a broadening smile, abandoning all thought of work, plotting my next fishing trip."
—Ted Williams, Conservation Editor, *Fly Rod & Reel*

"Delves into the origins and culture of fly-fishing with a bibliophilic glee. . . . A clarifying collection of facts and essays that connects the modern fly-fisherman with the very root of his art and sport."
—Jamie McAlister, *BookPage*

"What allows Schullery to rise a cut above most fishing writers, aside from the fact that he writes with grace and brevity, is his deflationary tactic. In a literature so abounding in snobs and reverse snobs, Schullery comes like a blast of fresh air, an iconoclast with an inclusive spirit that Whitman would have admired."
—*Kirkus Reviews*

"Schullery is one of the finest authors of natural history and fly-fishing currently writing."
—*Library Journal*

ROYAL
COACHMAN

The Lore and Legends
of Fly-Fishing

PAUL SCHULLERY

Illustrated by Eldridge Hardie

A FIRESIDE BOOK
PUBLISHED BY SIMON & SCHUSTER
NEW YORK LONDON SYDNEY SINGAPORE

FIRESIDE
Rockefeller Center
1230 Avenue of the Americas
New York, NY 10020

First Fireside Edition 2000
FIRESIDE and colophon are
registered trademarks of Simon & Schuster, Inc.
Designed by Karolina Harris
Manufactured in the United States of America
1 3 5 7 9 10 8 6 4 2
The Library of Congress has cataloged the Simon & Schuster edition as follows:
Schullery, Paul.
Royal coachman : the lore and legends of fly-fishing / Paul Schullery.
p.   cm.
1. Fly-fishing. 2. Flies, Artificial. I. Title.
SH456.S3225   1999
799.1'24—dc21   98-31760 CIP
ISBN 0-684-84246-7
0-684-86597-1 (Pbk)

*This book is dedicated to Bud Lilly,
a great fisherman, conservationist, and friend.
In a world where the very concept of hero
has been either cynically discarded or commercialized
into triviality, it's good to know someone who still
measures up to an earlier and higher
meaning of the word.*

CONTENTS

*I shall be content to write the rambling, idle, quite unpractical
sort of book about fishing that I myself like to read by the fire in
winter when the brooks are sealed, or by the stream on drowsy
noons—winding into and through the inexhaustible lore of angling
as a lazy brook goes through a meadow where the grass is heavy and
the reeds are high, pausing and deepening here and there but soon
running free again with a glitter of sun on the stickle.*

ODELL SHEPARD

One

ALL THE YOUNG MEN
WITH FLY RODS

F LY-FISHING is this great adventure we have in a thousand little episodes. Fly-fishing is our chance to embrace the unmanufactured, to earn something honestly, and to give ourselves over entirely and passionately to a pursuit that is in some mystifying way both irrelevant and important. Fly-fishing drives us nuts and keeps us sane. And, like any other addiction—any other so-called pastime that can take your soul away—given the chance, fly-fishing becomes something very much like a way of life.

Some years ago I was in Berkeley, visiting with Professor A. Starker Leopold, who, though best known as a leading thinker in the world of wildlife management, was also an avid fly fisherman. In discussing a young fly fisherman friend of his,

Starker said that, "He's spending a lot of time in Alaska guiding and having a great time, but I worry about his future." In that one statement he summed up the bemusement many feel at the sight of this or that bright young person who, for reasons many of us sympathize with, has chucked most of life's traditional responsibilities to become a trout bum.

Many things Starker said have stuck with me, but I often find myself wondering about that statement, partly because, though I didn't admit it to him then, I saw myself more or less in the same position as his young friend. At the time of my acquaintance with Starker, during the last years before his death in 1983, I gave all outward signs of being a solid grown-up: a full-time job, pursuit of respectable publication projects, and commitment to various good causes. But my closest friends and family knew better; I was a plainclothes trout bum. I still am, and as the years pass, even I begin to worry about my future.

Apparently there is some question about what a trout bum is. Until recently I thought it was a pretty straightforward thing, but then I read Gary LaFontaine's foreword to John Gierach's excellent book *Trout Bum* and found my identity challenged. *Trout Bum* was the first modern book-length testament of a confirmed and self-described trout bum, and so I suppose it isn't surprising that there should be some problems with definition. But having known what I was for a long time before Gary wrote about me, it was still a shock to find he didn't think I qualified for trout bumship. Here is how he sees it:

> No one under the age of thirty qualifies as a trout bum. The whippersnapper living along a stream, or traveling from river to river, isn't a bum because he isn't committed to a way of life— he's on an adventure. He hasn't actually rejected such encumbrances as a wife, children, and house payments. He just hasn't

gotten around to considering them yet. But the thirty- or forty-year-old man (or, of course, woman), who commercially ties just enough flies, guides just enough clients, or sweeps just enough floors so that he can spend the rest of his hours on the water is a derelict in the eyes of the world who should confess his sins.

I can't buy any of this. I came to appreciate the trout bum life when I was in my early twenties, and I will not be denied my place on account of some arbitrarily established age limit. I wasn't "on an adventure" except in the sense that life is, at its best, always an adventure. I know I was a trout bum, because some people who were very important to me would have called me that if only they'd heard the term. By the time I was thirty I'd generated more bemusement and outright consternation among those good-hearted souls who worry about the future of others than many far older trout bums have. It was, as the shrinks might say, a life choice, wrapped up in my enthusiasm for natural history and wilderness (I was also a nature bum and a national park bum). Having gotten a full-time job when I was twenty-nine ("Aha," Gary would say) didn't change anything fundamental. I knew I was the same. On any given day I would rather be out fishing somewhere, and on any given day I had the freedom to make the choice to go. Knowing I was that free made it okay to choose not to go—quite yet. It still is not a fantasy for me, on the slightly less depressing side of fifty, to say that one of these days I'm going back on the road. I mean it. It's something I figured out a long time ago, and I couldn't ever lose sight of it completely. That's how life choices are.

I'd say the same thing about trout bums that is said about marines: there is no such thing as an ex-trout bum.

Knowing all that, I had to wonder why Gary was setting up

this Gierach fellow as the type specimen for all trout bums. Sure, John writes great books (so does Gary, for that matter), and sure, *Trout Bum* is a superb statement of the joys of the fly-fishing life. But as I read John's book I was troubled: What's this?—this guy actually *owns his house!* What sort of bum owns a house? Besides, he doesn't just commit himself to fishing, he takes himself out of the anonymity of the true, single-minded trout devotee by writing about it. He compromises his calling to become that most risky of sporting types, The Expert. Worse, he succeeds at it and produces instructional writing every bit as fine and funny as his essays. He doesn't seem any more purely a bum than I, who literally hate home ownership, and who put my writing effort into suggesting that I am anything but an expert.

So Gary is welcome to consider John the ideal trout-bum role model, but I think we need to be more open-minded about who else gets the same label. John didn't invent this lifestyle; trout bumhood has a long tradition. Even Theodore Gordon, who, according to somewhat idealized tradition, forsook the life of an urban businessman back at the turn of the century and undertook American fly-fishing's most famous idyll in the Catskills, was only doing what many had done before him. There have always been at least a few people willing to give up a lot in order to do justice to trout fishing.

The first record I can find of a trout bum in this country (there are earlier examples in British fishing writing) is a man named John Dennison. In the August 1832 issue of *The American Turf Register and Sporting Magazine*, Dennison was described by a correspondent who signed himself "Leather Stocking":

... John Dennison, alias, Johnny Trout, as he is familiarly called by the sportsmen, has been a trout fisher for twenty odd years, and has probably killed more trout than any one person in the United States. He has been and is employed, by the frequenters of the trout streams from Boston and all parts of the country, to show them the sly places where the fish congregate, and also to catch them a mess, when all their exertions have failed; and now that he has grown old in their service, a gentleman from Boston, (to his praise be it said) has built him a snug house, where he is happy to furnish the waders of the brook with rods and lines for a moderate compensation.

Would that modern trout bums could count on such a retirement; a lot fewer futures would be worried about today. Where are the gentlemen from Boston when we need them?

And I have another question. How did we ever get from this view of trout fishermen as at imminent risk of social dissolution, and of trout fishing as little better than a social disease, to today? How did the image get turned around so completely? What is it that makes fly-fishing so commercially marketable and trendy now, at the same time that we fly fishermen are such a fractious, lampoonable crowd? Few things seem more improbable here in the final, nervous hours of the twentieth century than that this intensely personal and oddly tradition-oriented sport, so long the province of obsessive loners and snooty grouches, should become fashionable. Who could have predicted that?

Trout bums have appeared in every generation of fishermen since Dennison's day. Perhaps what makes them so little remembered is that, at least until recently, most of them seemed to accept society's judgment of them as wastrels and good-for-nothings. Besides, perhaps what made society judge them that way is that a lot of them were.

Consider a man immortalized in the neglected but charming book *Bodines; or Camping on the Lycoming,* a minor classic of early Pennsylvania angling writing published in Philadelphia in 1879. The author, Thad Up De Graff, did his trout fishing in northern Pennsylvania, on the venerable Lycoming, and devoted a chapter to a character named Shorty, known as the "Shark of the Stream," and also known as a fly fisherman who even in those dark, immoderate days was able to shock his fellow anglers with his excessive kills:

> He was a man of about fifty years of age, short of stature, with a small, round head, densely covered with long, shaggy, unkempt hair—an equal mixture of auburn and gray—while whiskers of the same bountiful supply and of like hue, almost concealed a pale and plump face. His eyes were blue and bright, mouth large, and well filled with tobacco-stained teeth that were exposed by the broad grin wrinkling his cheeks. He wore a black coat, threadbare, and abundantly patched, while his trousers (what was left of them) exposed a once white shirt, from front and rear, and a well-bronzed skin at the knees. This uniform was topped out with a black slouch hat, profusely ornamented with artificial flies, which seemed to have been collected from the back leaves of the fly-books of all the fishermen who had visited this stream for the past few years.

Shorty was what might charitably be called a type; he lived on the edge of the law and well outside the accepted rules of sportsmanship. He was a market-fisherman, and a liar of natural style and considerable dignity. He fulfilled all the needs of the prevailing stereotype of the crafty, unprincipled hick.

But it is in considering Shorty and others like him that I find Gary LaFontaine's definition of a trout bum most unsuccessful. That Shorty had a house, a wife, and six children does not weaken his claim to bumhood but strengthens it. Here he was, fifty years old (about my age, I flinch to notice), with all these apparent responsibilities, and he didn't give in. He didn't even run away to escape them; he just ignored them and went fishing. That's commitment.

It's also nearly too much for modern genteel sensibilities. Shorty compels us to ask the question: How do we keep clear the distinction between someone who fishes so much he becomes a bum, and someone who is just a bum who likes to fish? It's not a simple question, especially if asked of the parents, former wives, or current friends of most modern trout bums.

But the very difficulty of the question makes my point: We don't dare overrestrict our definition of this interesting type of person. By its very nature—requiring creative looseness, obstinate perseverance when confronted by peer disapproval, and diffidence in the face of potential security—trout bumhood encourages new directions.

This isn't easy to do, you know. Lots of people throw away perfectly good marriages or abandon promising careers to do something their friends agree is monstrously stupid, but giving up security is a lot easier than living without it indefinitely, the way trout bums do. Not just anybody can live in a station wagon for months at a time, or tolerate plain oatmeal with instant milk and no sugar for dinner every night for a week. Given the demands the lifestyle makes on a person, we should not be surprised that there are many kinds of trout bums (even rich ones, though we rarely apply the word "bum" to anyone with money). Nor should we risk short-circuiting any new evolutionary possibilities by overdefinition.

So I suggest that for once let's resist the stereotype. How many times have we read of the wise old angler or outdoorsman who lives on the edge of town, avoided by the good citizens and loved by the little boys he teaches to fish and hunt? We've even had enduring caricatures of him—a sure sign of a stereotype in the last stages of ossification—such as Patrick McManus's marvelous old phony, Rancid Crabtree. Let's not reduce the modern trout bum, a creature of great mobility and ingenuity, to the sort of banal simplicity of image we've applied to his ancestors. The very existence of John Gierach's book, capably celebrating an unorthodox lifestyle, poses a kind of threat to the trout bum as a social outsider; literary recognition of this sort will lead unavoidably to increasing respect for these rebellious souls. Let's not make the preservation of the species any harder than it is.

The modern trout bum is in fact a robust new strain of this old and long-unaltered species. Most of the new ones display no behavioral similarities to traditional bum imagery, commonly applied to lost souls and shiftless vagrants; instead of being dull, ignorant, and slothful, modern trout bums tend to be bright, educated, and passionately energetic about their chosen life. They will probably end up no worse off than the rest of the world, and in the end they will have a lot to remember even if they have little to show. Some will drift off into real trades, some will hang on near the edges of fly-fishing, maybe even opening a little fly shop and going nuts for a few years trying to make a business out of a religion. Some will leave it all behind and become computer programmers or attorneys. The gifted few, like Gierach, will take the time to write about it and may risk their hard-won independence by becoming a part of fly-fishing's literary establishment. Most others will just go on enjoying the life. But very few will ever go hungry, because, like all other forms of social vagrancy, trout bumhood well practiced breeds resourcefulness.

Think of the ones you've seen: the lean young men with a competent look about them and road maps in their eyes, so different from one another in personality and background, but so similar in their one shared passion. If their obvious self-assurance doesn't convince you that they need no one to worry about them, think of this: Even as they live today, even as you've seen them out on streams all over the country, crawling out of rusting, home-customized vans, or tying flies in front of a tent somewhere, you've never seen one get hungry enough that he had to eat a trout. Shorty should have had it so good.

For me it began in Yellowstone. In 1972, I started my first summer there as a ranger-naturalist. Outfitted with a borrowed fly rod and one small box of flies, I embarked on a great long journey of discovery, alternating frustration with delight, exasperation with exhilaration, as I wandered up and down the park's famous and little-known trout streams. Those streams were great teachers and even greater friends. They still are.

It was all part of a much greater journey, of course. Yellowstone took hold of me so completely that I suppose I will never be free of its pull, or ever want to be. I applied my training in history to the park's unique saga as a centerpiece of the American conservation movement and eventually became park historian on an occasional basis. The year before coming to Yellowstone, I had tried one brief quarter of graduate school but found it so oppressive and unfulfilling that I bailed out, deciding that there had to be a better way to learn. Yellowstone provided that way. Between my summer and winter stints at Yellowstone, I returned intermittently to graduate school, eventually taking seven years to complete a two-year M.A. program in American history and writing my thesis on Yellowstone's wonderful archives, the administrative record of the park dating all the way back to the 1870s.

So I explored the park's history with the same enthusiasm with which I explored its streams and trails, and the two pursuits grew into one and gave me a sense of direction that was a total surprise. I had pretty much expected to drift through life, trying this and that, but probably not latching onto any one thing—another, less focused kind of bumhood that probably became impossible for me by the time my first summer in Yellowstone ended and the park had hold of my heart.

But much of my time wasn't spent in Yellowstone or in school, and it was then that I learned the joys of being a trout bum in its purest form: on long, rambling trips to new rivers, with no known deadlines except some remote day, months away, when I had to be back at work or school.

There is one piece of property that the modern trout bum finds almost essential for full exercise of the art these days, and that's a reliable car. Some modern trout bums can practice their creed from one spot, but most of us need more mobility. I certainly did. For some reason, I have always kept a simple "auto log" for each car I owned. As I look through the log I used back then, it tells much more of a story than would seem possible in what is really only a list of gasoline prices, dates, and places. But even to the casual fisherman some of the names that appear would be familiar and might suggest the car's real mission: Key West, Grayling, and lots of places that end in "falls," "creek," or "river." And to the more serious fisherman there is every indication of an odyssey here: Steamboat, Livingston, Jackson, Roscoe, Homestead. And for the absolute angling fanatic, the single-minded pilgrim, there is the final proof, the harder-to-learn names that say "Here, far from anywhere you'd think, here is the real mainstream": Glide, Agness, Mio, Marblemount. Of course these names mean the most to me, who entered them all in the journal so faithfully, for no good reason except that I thought some day I'd be glad I did.

And I am glad, but not for quite the reason I expected. I find that I'm as grateful for the reminders of the places *between* the places I was going, all the strong Western names—Crow Agency, Wolf Creek, Elk Point, Red Lodge. Or the fertile blue-mountain names of the older frontiers—Sweetwater, Greenup, Mount Pisgah, Peaks of Otter. Getting there was more than half the fun; getting there was the reason for wanting to go. I was always most restless before I started and after I arrived, as if something in me, even when I was fishing, was anxious to be out and moving again, looking to the next spot. Anticipation itself became sport, and travel became the final manifestation of anticipation.

My car was a light-blue Volkswagen Super Beetle. I bought it in Tucson in 1972, trading in the crumpled remains of an earlier Beetle that I'd flipped and totaled a few days before in Mexico. The new one got its first servicing in Colorado, its second in Ohio, and its third in Montana. This was routine for six years.

I removed the bottom half of the backseat, so that the top half would fold down flat and hold more books, clothes, and fishing tackle. Often I removed the front passenger seat as well, and converted the right side of the car into a bunk of sorts; that allowed me a level of self-sufficiency not usually associated with such small cars. It was good sleeping, and cheap almost beyond belief. Every week or so on a long trip, I'd have to clean out all the little spaces into which loose change, fly boxes, film, and sandwiches would fall. When I finally sold the car, I suspected that if someone cared to look they would still find some film canisters, maybe a few flies embedded in the upholstery, possibly even an emergency five-dollar bill squirreled away and forgotten under a corner of the floor mat.

The car was resold almost instantly, within a few hours of my dropping it off, and I imagine that if the new owner was at all observant, he found plenty of other fisherman's "sign" as well. I kept a small selection of flies, assorted rejects and retirees from my fly box, poked into the padding of the dashboard by the right wing window; he'd have had to wonder what the little holes there were caused by. He would have immediately felt the rough places on the outer rim of the steering wheel, where I attached my fly-tying vise on rainy days in camp. The first time he looked in the rearview mirror, he must have noticed how the back window was marred from the continual rubbing of aluminum rod cases. The right sun visor, which he would have found in the trunk, had a fly attached to it that I just now remember I'd wanted to get; my brother Steve tied it for me, and it caught an amazing number of fish, amazing mostly because I lose flies so fast. I have a feeling about that car that is more than gratitude. It took me so many wonderful places that I can't feel otherwise.

It was a quest. That strong a word might seem pretentious or silly if you've never been on one, but I think most gut-hooked fishermen will know what I mean. At times, for all my general state of impoverishment (each fly purchased was a long-considered investment, weighed against the price of bologna or a milkshake), there was this feeling that I was doing something,

well, important. Hardly anybody else cared, but I knew it mattered.

Among my Yellowstone seasonal ranger friends were several
who worked two parks, one in summer and another in winter;
a whole group of them conducted a ragtag migration in aging
microbuses, back and forth between Wyoming and south
Florida every year—between Yellowstone and the Everglades.
We were part of a sprawling social network of such park people, which meant we were part of a sort of informal hospitality
system as well. If you were willing to live like we did, and
loved the same things we did, there were many beautiful
places around the country where you could usually find a
friendly face and a vacant floor upon which to throw your
sleeping bag. One winter, that meant I had to make the long
drive to Everglades National Park, which was even more of a
wonder than I'd been told. I was thrilled by the birdlife, hiked
through the epiphytic forest, photographed gators without
end, and stayed up late playing guitar and singing with equally
blessed friends.

And I fished. By now I owned more than one fly rod, including a hefty old Fenwick fiberglass 9-footer for a 10-weight
line—a rod so stout that my brother, a fly fisherman of more
delicate sensitivities, referred to it as the "barge pole." With
this rod, I briefly hooked a snook in a canal along the Tamiami
Trail, I landed a truly ferocious 12-inch barracuda on some
anonymous flat south of Miami, and, miracle of miracles, I
caught a bonefish.

A ranger I met in the Everglades told me to try the pilings
along an old roadbed that stretched out from the shore of No-
Name Key, where he thought I might find a yellowtail (a saltwater species whose form I could not even imagine) that would

take a fly. I drove partway down the Keys the night before so I could get an early start, because I was having a hard time with the intense heat and humidity so abruptly encountered after my drive from the Rockies. But the sun was already hot when I parked the car and walked out on the spit of land—an old road to nowhere—and started casting.

I was using a floating shooting head, and the pull of the line against the light running line was some comfort, but there were no yellowtails to be had. All I got were a few nibbles from the needlefish. As usual, I'd done some reading, so I knew that the tide (what an odd thing to suddenly have to worry about, for one so recently come from the mountains) was all wrong; the pilings I was supposed to cast to were all but dry.

By 9:00 the sun had achieved that brassy oppressive brightness I'd read about in novels of the tropics, and I was ready to quit before my predictable midday vertigo hit. It was a long, hot drive back to Flamingo, where I was staying. Then some clammers went by in a small boat and told me there was a group of snappers below them, but it was too far and too deep for me to reach, so I waded from the shallows, started to leave, and took one more look around. About 60 feet off the end of the spit, in water only a few feet deep, there was a small light-green patch surrounded by the darker bottom. It was an easy cast with my rig, so I waded a few yards out and winged a big yellow Lefty's Deceiver over it and slowly retrieved it.

The strike didn't come over the patch, but I suspect now that the fish was in the patch and followed the fly until it was about 40 feet from me, then hit. It was more a sudden resistance than a strike, but I responded with the predictable vigor of a large, overexcited young man, hauling back on the rod and setting the hook deeply into whatever creature this was. This was all new, you understand, and I intended to participate fully.

The fish headed out across the little bay, more or less toward Galveston. I suppose it was because of the depth of the water that the run wasn't like those described in the books, in which bonefish race across the flats so fast the line hums as it cuts through the water. This was not a violent run, or even a steady run. The fish just kept going, sometimes slower, sometimes faster. I had somehow, through luck, I suppose, cleared the loose line around my feet; it was gone right away, and then the rest of the running line and then the backing began to slip away too.

The run seemed to go on for a long time, so long that I had time to wander back out of the shallows and talk to myself about it. I hadn't seen any of this backing since it was put on the reel. After a while, I asked myself if the fish could really be going to take all the backing, or if it wasn't a fish at all but some other animal. I didn't really know much about what all might live around here.

After another while, not long before bare spool would have shown, probably close to 200 yards into the run, the fish stopped. I had by now inventoried what little I knew about how saltwater fish fight. Barracuda were supposed to be jumpers, so I ruled them out. As I began to reel, I thought for the first time about bonefish—not that I might have one, but that it was said you could sometimes reel them almost all the way in before they began their second run.

I had a lot of reeling to do and was hard at it when I looked out over the ocean and saw that my line was coming back toward me in a big circle. The fish had turned and was making a grand loop to the left and back, much faster than I could reel my single-action Medallist to keep up. As the front end of the fly line approached shore (whoever heard of such a thing?), I was able to visually follow it, then look about 10 feet out from it to the end of the leader, where the fish was. What with refraction, it seemed a long, lean thing, distinctly sharklike at first glance, but the books said sharks were not good sight feeders, so I doubted it was a shark.

As it continued its loop, the fish actually passed about 30 feet in front of me, trailing a huge circle of line as it crossed under the backing I was still furiously cranking in. I could see the big fly trailing from the side of its mouth. The fish tilted a bit, and its side flashed like a mirror in the sun. Now I realized that I might indeed have a bonefish. I became more excited.

Trailing the heavy shooting head, the fish continued on along the shore, then out again, and when I got the line tight, it made another run, about 100 feet. I followed to the end of the spit, and with the confidence borne of a 15-pound test leader, I began turning the fish, snubbing off the weaker runs, until the fish was circling quietly only 20 or 30 feet from shore. Now that it seemed I might actually land it, I got a little more cautious with my pressure, and finally did land it by backing up and sliding it ashore. I was talking more or less continually now, to the air, to myself, and to the gorgeous 7-pound bonefish lying quietly on the sand. I became more excited.

It was strangely easy to land. I knew better, and I was pretty sure that killing the fish was bad manners and a waste, but I had to do something with this fish for a little while, if only carry it back to the car and take a picture of it. I yelled at the clammers, now some distance off, and held up the fish, but I couldn't tell if they heard or saw.

I hurried back to the car, laid the fish on the ground, and photographed it a couple of times, with my fly rod and reel lying next to it for scale. I measured it, weighed it, and spent some time studying it. It was much broader-shouldered than I'd imagined; the photos of bonefish in books and magazines are almost always from the side, so you get no idea of how thick the fish is from side to side. I talked to myself and to the fish. I studied that peculiar grinding structure in the mouth that allows them to crush crab shells so easily, and I gaped at the overall grandness of the fish, wishing I could find someone to take my picture with it.

I've often marveled at the timing of this. Just then, on this isolated key with no houses anywhere around, at the deadest end of the road, a little delivery truck pulled up. The driver, a Cuban as near as I could tell, stepped out. He spoke even less English than I spoke Spanish, but we understood each other. He'd apparently missed a turn and was lost. I wanted a picture. I handed him my little Instamatic, he took a couple of quick snapshots. He seemed slightly interested in the fish, so I offered it to him—held it out and said something lame and simple. He became more excited. Neither of us knew if this thing was even edible, but it was clear both of us knew that was an important question to get answered before he took it home to his family, so we went through a minute or so of making sure he had the name right so he could ask around. I'd say "Bonefish," and he'd repeat "Bahnfeesh," and we'd go back and forth that way. We thanked each other, then nodding and smiling and waving a lot, he put the fish in his truck and drove off.

This was when the sense of quest again took hold. I drove my little fishing car on out to Key West, just for a look, then made the long drive up the Keys to the Everglades, and all along the way I dealt with a mood of half contentment about what I'd done, half anxiety that it wouldn't be complete until I'd shared it. So I sent a postcard to my friends in Yellowstone. It said something like this:

Bonefish

25 inches

7 pounds

Rejoice, O Camelot, for I have found the Grail.

My car was a pretty happy place right then.

I got the car stuck only once, on a sandy beach along the Rogue River in Oregon. The local deputy sheriff winched me out with his pickup truck, refusing payment with, "Forget it, I must pull thirty people out of here every summer." The only time the car ever came to real harm was in Washington, when a lumberjack backed his truck into it and smashed the rear deck. It was the only two-car accident I know of with no witnesses. I was in a nearby campground building, paying too much for a lukewarm shower, when I heard the truck's roaring, unmuffled engine, then a faint crunch that the driver did not hear, being too close to the engine himself. Luckily he lived right there, and I just waited a few hours until he came home.

The car came near to greater harm one day along the Madison in Yellowstone. I'd parked and waded upstream about a quarter of a mile and was standing up to my aspirations in the river when I heard the rumble of a rock slide high up the canyon wall above the car. From where I stood I could see large boulders bouncing down toward the forest-lined road directly above where I'd parked. With a feeling of detachment equaled only by the most walleyed television viewer, I waited to see if any of the rocks would make it through the trees to my car. Some of them, the ones that looked bigger than the car, were lined up perfectly. As I watched, one by one they crashed into some tree or other and were stopped or deflected. I couldn't see any of this; all I could see was the top of a tree, here and there, suddenly lurch and crack as a boulder slammed into it, and all I could do was wait for the metallic crash and tinkle of a direct hit. The car was on its own.

The crash never came, and later I was calm enough to be impressed by my unmoving reaction to the whole episode. After all, what sense would it have made for me to go sloshing across the river toward the rock slide, yelling "My car! My car!" and waving my arms? I surely couldn't have reached the car in time to do anything more than get squashed myself.

Another time, as I was coming back from a day's fishing on a blessedly little-known Wyoming stream, the voltage regulator went out just at dark, and I drove the last few miles of twisting, cliff-hugging mountain road with my brother leaning out the passenger window, lighting the road with a flashlight. He kept interrupting my deep concern for the car's welfare with silly remarks about what a "swell adventure" this all was. That was the closest the car ever came to failing me, and the closest I ever came to fratricide, or at least sibling abuse, my brother having no feel at all for how personally I took the car's sufferings.

But thinking back, I find there were few times the car gave me cause to worry. It was so reliable that it became a major part of my life, a part that means even more when I see an occasional logbook entry in a more delicate hand that reminds me that not all the trips were made alone. But even those that were solo rarely seemed more lonely than I needed them to be. The car was as much a home as any building. After a long, embarrassing day of steelhead fishing, I'd retire to my car with, appropriately, a copy of *Don Quixote* and read of other hopeless quests. Then, after a search of the local radio stations (back then, the quality of the fishing was almost always inversely re-

lated to the number of stations) for the day's great road an-
thems—Gordon Lightfoot's "Carefree Highway" and Jim
Croce's "I've Got a Name" were my highest hopes—I'd take
one last look around to make sure that my campsite was bear-
and raccoon-proof and crawl into my bunk. Then, settled into
my nest of rumpled sleeping bags, festering groceries, tattered
field guides, and mixed laundry, looking up through the rear
window to the broken canopy of Douglas fir, I would think
fondly of my friends and family and consider where I was going
to go next.

Two

THE FISHERMAN'S CHAUCER

T H E idea of fishing secrets—of arcane lore that will help us catch a fish—has always been a driving force behind fishing-book publication. One can't spend as much time failing as fishermen do without nurturing some mighty dream of better days; the magic that attracts us to fishing books is the revealed secret, whether ancient and long lost or recently discovered. Though we pride ourselves on our pragmatism, at times most of us harbor a very nearly occult obsession with some imagined higher awareness, a state of knowing that will give us the right lure, the right bait, the right rod, the right sequence of profanity—whatever it is that we're plainly not doing now will be revealed to us, and we will become that most envied and lionized of fishermen,

The Expert. (Later I will tell you about actual experts with whom I have fished; they really do catch at least twice as many fish as I do, which is to say that they spend 98, rather than 99, percent of their time catching nothing.)

Those of us who pay attention to such things recently celebrated the 500th anniversary of the tradition of seeking out secrets. In 1496, the printer Wynken de Worde, of St. Albans, Hertfordshire, published a new edition of *The Boke of St. Albans,* a compendium of advice on field sports first published ten years earlier. To increase its popularity, he added "The Treatise on Fishing with an Angle," placing this remarkable essay in the larger work, he explained, to prevent its falling into "the hands of each idle person which would desire it if it were imprinted alone by itself. . . ." The Treatise's quality of information apparently was regarded rather like the amazing abilities of a modern superhero, who is required to pledge not to use his powers for evil. Gentlemen who could afford to buy the bigger book must have been seen as a better bet to behave themselves than the riffraff who could buy a little pamphlet. This 1496 edition of the book, including the Treatise, which was not published separately until the early 1530s, has long been heralded as our first fishing book.

The Treatise defined the full character of modern sportfishing, for which we have honored it even beyond its considerable merit. The late Arnold Gingrich, founder of *Esquire* magazine and author of several companionable fly-fishing books, said that the book's supposed author, Dame Juliana Berners, "is to angling literature as Chaucer is to English literature, representing to all practical intents and purposes the very beginning."

Well, no. The Treatise has provided us with a handy symbolic point of origin, but it's not the beginning of fishing literature. Recent research has established that sportfishing (and flyfishing, that being the specialty most glorified by later writers) traditions flourished and produced written texts here and there in Europe for centuries prior even to the appearance of the various known manuscript fragments of the Treatise that existed by the mid-1400s.

But the Treatise is still extraordinary for its completeness as a tract of technique and attitude. It dealt with the society, as well as with the practice, of fishing. Reading it today, we are struck by its modern message, once we have modernized its spelling. Not only are we told that "at the least" (read, "even if you don't catch anything") the fisherman can count on all the joys of nature ("he hath his wholesome walk and merry at his ease, [and] a sweet air of the sweet savor of the meadow flowers that makes him hungry. He hears the melodious harmony of birds. . . ."), but also that the perplexing challenge of catching the fish will make success all the finer. Sport was obviously a well-formed notion five hundred years ago, involving not merely the harvest of wild animals but their harvest according to recognized norms and restrictions that often made harvest harder and thereby made the sport finer. There is also emphasis on fishing manners: ask permission to fish on private land, "break no man's hedges in going about your sport," and be moderate in your take (perhaps the author-expert's ego showed through when noting that excessive take could easily happen "if you do in every point as this present treatise shows you").

The technical advice was exceptional too, a densely informative text not only about fish natural history but also about how to make tackle, choose baits and flies, and determine the right time to fish. Several of the Treatise's twelve flies are among the most famous of the tens of thousands of fly patterns that have been invented. British fishing writer John Waller Hills, in his *A History of Fly Fishing for Trout* (1921), correctly proclaimed that the Treatise "set a stamp on angling literature which has lasted to our time," which was a restrained way of saying that for two or three centuries it was shamelessly parroted by later writers.

We have taken this literary tradition a long way and asked more of it than it might fairly be relied upon to give us. For example, ask any modern fishing writer who dabbles in history what fishing was like in 1500, and he or she will cite the Treatise, describe the various techniques and tackle prescribed in its pages, and feel pretty good about being able to give you such an authoritative answer. But, though we know that the Treatise did have a great influence on a few later fishing writers in subsequent centuries, we have very little way of measuring, or even guessing, how widely its advice was practiced by regular fishermen at the time of its publication. It and its earlier manuscript forms probably represent the thinking and the practices of several people over the course of a century or so, but it's a big leap from the activities of that little group to what was being done on hundreds of British streams and lakes by thousands of fishermen, many of whom were either illiterate or far removed from the limited circulation of such writings as the Treatise.

I prefer to assume that fishermen then, as now, had a healthy competitive attitude about these things: that some lifelong fly fisher 50 miles from St. Albans (or wherever the compiler of the Treatise lived), if introduced to the Treatise's advice, say on how to tie the stone fly, would have been just as likely to laugh and say words to the effect of, "Well, some might like that, but that wing will never work, and the yellow belly is all wrong." These differences of opinion are not just part of fishing; they are part of human nature. Opinions on fishing, then as now, must have depended upon many things, including the angler's personality, local traditions, and variations in local environments (different insects or water conditions, for example). The Treatise does provide us with a precious, rare window into another time, but we don't know that it's giving us a typical or even a very wide view. One book, even if it had several authors or compilers, could hardly be a comprehensive survey of an entire nation's fishing habits and attitudes. Even Ray Bergman, with telephones, years of travel, and the common touch, couldn't achieve that.

But for all the information in the Treatise, the heart of its legend lies in its authorship. Fishing writers have given historians fits by freely accepting that someone named Juliana Berners wrote it; to the leading scholars of the subject, her name is at best a bibliographical crutch. Though modern reseachers are providing us with some stimulating theories about a person by that name and someday may actually find the real person, hard evidence of her existence is slight, and evidence that she had anything to do with writing the Treatise is nonexistent. In the end of the *hunting* section of the *Boke* is the phrase "Explicit Dam Iulyans Barnes in her boke of huntyng." This is not quite a byline, but scholars recognize that it might mean that the hunting section was based on, or quoted from, some other work by Barnes, most likely in manuscript form. (However, the best scholarship suggests that she probably didn't write the hunting material either.)

The *Boke of St. Albans* never says who wrote the fishing material. By the mid-1500s, though, it too was attributed to Barnes, who became "Berners" at the hand of many later writers. Over the next two centuries, a fanciful biography of her emerged that portrayed her as the original sportswoman, skilled in all the blood sports, what one historian called a "Diana/Minerva image." Generations of historians have failed to find proof of the existence of any of her various proposed personae, which have included nun, prioress, teacher, noblewoman, and various combinations of these.

Meanwhile, fishing writers continue merrily retelling half-baked stories in praise of her. Even those who know better still apologetically refer to the book as hers. As John Waller Hills put it (to the evident agreement of almost all later fishing writers): "I shall treat her as author until a better claimant appears, for it is awkward to have to cite an anonymous book." This, too, doesn't measure up to scholarly practice. Led by medievalist Richard Hoffmann, who in a series of pathbreaking scholarly papers has single-handedly rewritten the early history of fly-fishing, historians want to know why it is so awkward to cite an anonymous book (it's done all the time) and why it's better to cite instead a fictional, if not mythical character. But as Hoffmann and others have pointed out, we are indeed in the realm of myth here. Fishing history, like most history, rests on a tangled web of belief systems, self-perceptions and romance, and mere facts just don't compete. After all, these are fishermen we're talking about.

This plot threatens to thicken, if not congeal entirely. In *Reel Women, the World of Women Who Fish* (1995), Lyla Foggia champions Berners by asking "Are we to believe that 500 years ago a woman would be credited with authoring a document she did not write—when it's extraordinary enough that a woman would be credited at all?" Of course, five hundred years ago, no one, man or woman, was credited with writing the Treatise, but Foggia's assertion reveals another element of the problem: gender. Implicit in Foggia's argument is sexism: that resistance to Berners's authenticity is the result of men refusing to admit that a woman was the author of the first book on this male-dominated sport.

Not that fishermen are not sexist—at times I think that, compared to other groups of men, they are disproportionately so—but you don't have to spend much time reading old fishing books to notice that, rather than resist the Berners claim, generations of angling writers have wholeheartedly embraced it, displaying a happy tokenism toward this safe, historically remote (all the more remote for possibly being a nun) woman.

Berners, or Barnes, survives for other, deeper reasons than evidence. She survives because she fills a role, giving an entire field of human activity a tidy origin. Juliana Berners is fishing's Eve. John McDonald, in his brilliant 1963 book *The Origins of Angling* (for every thousand fishing books that deserve to be out of print, there is one magnificent one like McDonald's that should be mandated to remain in print by law), "plausibly proved" that she was not the author of the Treatise but went on to conclude that "in elevating our recognition of her from legend to true myth, we have perhaps provided anglers with what they really want."

Now that "her" book has been supplanted by innumerable others, it may be in this mythic realm that Juliana Berners serves us best. She exemplifies fishing's mystery and thereby leaves room for hope. The Treatise personifies the original expert—the first to publish a handbook and thus the first to offer promise of relieving the fisherman's bewilderment.

Furthermore, even the Treatise, the supposed Old Testament of the sport, tantalizes us with lost lore, at one point vaguely citing unnamed "bokes of credence" as among the sources for its knowledge. McDonald tends to disregard this vague acknowledgment of even earlier works on angling, pointing out that "in view of the medieval fondness for citing authorities wherever possible, it seems likely that most of the treatise was written from personal experience and oral tradition." I agree that most of the Treatise was probably based on oral tradition, but McDonald risks slighting what might be an important heads-up to us; the Treatise could really be telling us that we have not yet seen everything there is to see in early fishing writing. I think that's almost certainly true; in little more than a decade, Richard Hoffmann has exposed an extraordinary variety of pre-1496 manuscript fishing material from various parts of Europe to the light of published day.

Even without Hoffmann's discoveries, we have excellent evidence that fishing books can vanish for centuries and then reappear. In 1954, the American bibliophile Karl Otto von Kienbusch purchased, from a London book dealer, what is so far the only known copy of *The Arte of Angling*, published in 1577 and lost to all memory. Almost certainly written by William Samuel, vicar of Godmanchester (the title page is missing from the Kienbusch copy), the book made quite a stir for its eyebrow-raising similarities to Izaak Walton's *The Compleat Angler* (1653). Walton's masterpiece was still a masterpiece, but its originality was not as pure as had been thought. And the text of *The Arte of Angling* provides us with even more reason to wonder what other old books may be out there. Near the end of the book's dialogue between an expert fisherman and a beginner (a dialogue form Walton apparently copied in his book), Piscator informs Viator that he will speak of other subjects "in my next edition."

Whether or not we ever find this next edition, or are even fortunate enough to find a surviving copy of any of the Treatise's alleged "bokes of credence" (note that the attribution is to multiple works), it seems overconfident to assume they do not exist. The possibility of their existence, in fact, is another satisfying part of the Treatise's legacy, leading hopeful angler-readers on fantasy explorations of neglected Old World archives, down dusty, poorly lit aisles and stacks, where some yet-undiscovered masterpiece lies waiting to help us catch a fish.

Three

EARLY AMERICAN TROUT FISHING

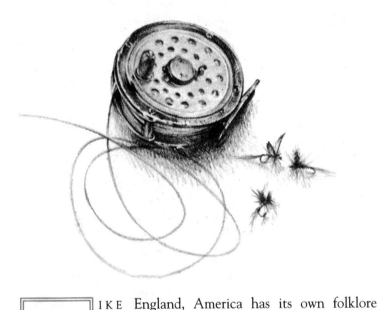

L IKE England, America has its own folklore about lost fishing books. In the first decades of the 1800s, when American sportsmen began to publish accounts of their hunting and fishing exploits, they did so mostly in a few magazines. By midcentury, American fishermen were reading the popular British writers and could even buy a few American books: J. V. C. Smith's *Natural History of the Fishes of Massachusetts* (1833) contained some discussion of fishing methods, but *Schreiner's Sporting Manual* (1841), John Brown's *American Angler's Guide* (1845) and his *Angler's Almanac* (1848), and Henry William Herbert's *Frank Forester's Fish and Fishing* (1851) were more useful instructional manuals, though often heavily derivative of the British writers for such specifics as fly patterns.

But as with the Treatise's "bokes of credence," there are some intriguing mysteries lingering from the early days of American fishing writing. The most perplexing, even exasperating, appear in the pages of British writer Robert Blakey's *Historical Sketches of Angling Literature of All Nations*, published in 1856. In this odd and perhaps even weird little book, Blakey, a widely published professor of logic at Queen's College, Belfast, presents something like an alternative universe for fishing-book enthusiasts, in which North America in the early 1800s was peopled with many fishing writers busily cranking out books:

> In the United States, and British America, angling literature has been cultivated with considerable ardour and success, particularly within the past thirty years. We find books on the subject in every section of this vast continent, where the English language is known, and English habits and amusements prevail, of more or less merit and pretensions, both in poetry and prose. In Connecticut, Vermont, New Hampshire, and the New England states generally, angling has been long a fashionable amusement among the literary and active minds of the country; and the whole of the continent, considerably beyond the White Mountains, has been visited by these zealous piscatory ramblers. Some have even penetrated into the unfrequented tributaries of the Missouri.

Blakey's account of this great flourishing publishing enterprise is nearly bizarre in its combination of specifics and infuriating vagueness. He tells us about a book called *On Angling*, supposedly published in Pittsburgh in 1852, and recites a poem from the book, entitled "On the Salmon Fly." He also cites another Pittsburgh book, *The Trout Fisher's Guide*, written by a

T. W. Dawson and published in 1850. Besides these two specific references, he gives us snippets from several other sources, some of which we know to be real, others of which are utterly untraceable.

But where is all this stuff? Ignoring his comments about all the books he doesn't name, no one has ever seen or again heard of the two Pittsburgh books, despite some energetic searching by leading Pennsylvania bibliographers over the years. That, and Blakey's other vague, confused ramblings, led the great British angling bibliographers Westwood and Satchell, in the 1901 edition of their *Bibliotheca Piscatoria,* to indignantly dismiss Blakey's book as "a slip-shod and negligent work, devoid of all real utility. A mere farrago of matter relevant and irrelevant, of indiscriminate sweepings from miscellaneous sources, of quotations incorrectly given and so-called original passages the vagueness and uncertainty of which rob them of all weight and value."

Though I always stop to admire such well-deserved and pungently eloquent criticism (I wish I'd said it, about a few modern books I know), I still wonder about those Pittsburgh books. Unless Blakey was just a psychopathic liar, there almost has to be something to those citations: some twisted little nugget of reality behind the florid imitation of erudition.

But as much as I would enjoy the discovery of these lost books, I have to admit that we fishermen have depended too exclusively on books for our appreciation of our past, and even if Blakey's mysterious books appeared, they could hardly illuminate much more of the life of early American anglers than the Treatise reveals about British fishing at the time of Columbus. The books just don't tell us enough.

In my book *American Fly Fishing: A History,* I grumped on for several pages about the extent to which we fishermen have misunderstood our past by relying solely on books. While professional historians (as opposed to fishing writers who write about history) of colonial America unanimously agree that, even in the 1600s, sportfishing was one of the most popular and widely enjoyed recreations throughout the colonies, fishing writers continue to say stunningly dumb things about how Americans before the early 1800s were too busy conquering the wilderness to fish except for survival rations between Indian wars. What has happened here is that fishing writers rely almost entirely on earlier fishing writers for their information, so they seem to reason something like this: There were no fishing writers publishing before 1800, therefore there must have been no fishing.

I didn't really expect my book to straighten this out; the nonexistence of sport fishermen in the New World before 1800 is as much a part of angling folklore as the existence of Juliana Berners. What I might hope for here, however, is to bring a little of that earlier world to life. It sounds to me like a pretty good world and a great place to fish.

Delegates to the Constitutional Convention in Philadelphia some two hundred years ago were by all accounts made miserable by the heat, and I suspect that more than one of them must have daydreamed, as the proceedings droned on, of taking a shady seat by some stream in the countryside thereabouts, rigging up his tackle, and going in search of trout.

Imagine you were one of those delegates, or one of their assistants or servants. Once you realized there was no escape from the work of the summer—at least no escape that would give you time to do justice to a good trout stream for a few days—you might have sought some brief diversion in at least getting ready to fish. You might have done what so many do when they only have a little time to devote to fishing: shop. Philadelphia was a good place to do that, so you could have excused yourself, pleading some humble mission of personal comfort, and hurried from the hall and over to Market Street. There you would have delivered yourself and your daydreams into the hands of Edward Pole, "Fishing-Tackle-Maker."

Speaking as a historian who has his own idea of treasure, I would rather spend an hour in Pole's shop back then with no money at all than be turned loose with $1,000 in any modern tackle shop in the world. Established, as near as we know, in the early 1770s, Pole's shop offered a full selection of gear to the avid anglers of southeastern Pennsylvania. He started advertising in *Dunlap's Pennsylvania Packet* in 1774, and by the year after the Declaration of Independence could boast an astonishing collection of stuff, the sort of list that makes modern tackle collectors dizzy with frustration that they cannot somehow be transported back there, buy one of everything, and bring it home.

The city-bound delegate could, according to Pole's advertisements, waggle rods of cedar, hazel, or dogwood. He could crank "wheels" for trolling, bass fishing, or trout (these, like most of the other tackle, were usually imported), and could even get a first look at the new "multiplier" reels with gearing to speed up the retrieve of line (really now, is that sporting?). He could study the lines, "cable laid, from large dolphin down to whiting, with hooks suitable from Bonettar [bonito?] to the smallest size." He could rummage among the weights, swivels, snaphooks, and floats (cork). And of course he could lose himself in the fly display, examining and choosing among the "artificial flies, moths, and hackles" Pole kept on hand.

If Pole himself happened to be behind the counter, our delegate might engage him in conversation over the quality of imported horsehair versus the local variety (which Pole bought when he could, apparently to have lines made from it), or hear the latest gossip about Pole's competitors in the Philadelphia tackle trade (Pole, of course, announced he was better stocked "than any other in the city"), or ask him how business was at The Wigwam, Pole's tavern on the edge of town along the Schuylkill river, where fishermen were welcomed and coddled between outings astream.

Pole's expression may have darkened at this last question; things were not going well at The Wigwam, and in 1788 he sold out, the tackle business going to one George Lawton, who was still prospering in 1803 (and advertising an even greater selection of tackle; the lures included "Artificial Flies, Moths, Hackles, Minnew, Chubbs, Grasshoppers, Dilderries, Frogs, Mice, Birds, Cadds, &c. for Trout and other Fishing"), the year in which he sold a fair amount of durable tackle to the Lewis and Clark expedition. How long Lawton lasted we do not know, but Pole, Lawton, and their competitors are revealing by their very existence. They tell us the extent to which Americans enjoyed sportfishing long before they are believed to have done so.

These first generations of sportfishers fascinate me. We know so little about the individuals. Fishing was not something to be written about then, much less published about. They left only incidental records—advertisements, journals, receipts, and the like (which is the chief reason why fishing writers ignored their existence, and most wrote fishing history as if it were merely the history of previous fishing writers). But people then were fishing what today we might think of as virgin waters, and imagine the excitement in that. (Of course the waters were not really virgin; people had been fishing them for at least ten thousand years. It would do us good to understand Native American concepts of sport better.)

I wonder, for example, about the Virginians, with their society so unlike Puritan Massachusetts; how many of those Virginia planters brought finely made tackle with them from the Old World? And what of the earliest settlers of Pittsburgh, who have left diary accounts of the incredible richness of the fishery resources around their primitive fort? Who first dragged a fly rod along on that westward migration? Or, in the far left field of my historical wonderings, what of settlers of Mexico and Spanish California? *The Little Treatyse on Fishing* (1539), by Fernando Basurto, a fascinating fly-fishing tract, established the extent to which Spanish sportfishing was based on a tradition independent of the British one. Did sportfishing find its way into the recreational interests of those first Euro-Californians?

These are not unanswerable questions. Sportfishing in the New World prior to 1800 is a wide-open field, just waiting for the attention of more historians. The evidence will not easily be found, but it is there for those willing to do the work. Just recently I came upon a 1687 estate list, published in a Pennsylvania history journal, which included in the property of James Harrison, master of Pennsbury Manor, "2 fishing Ceanes and a pasell of Lines." Whenever I see a mention of tackle like this ("ceanes" are "canes," a term that was sometimes used even to describe higher-quality rods as well as "poles"), I wish I could know more: What did he fish for? What was his favorite bait? Did he frequent the trout streams, or stick with the warm ponds, or take potluck in the Delaware River itself? Early American angling will for a long time cause those of us who care about fishing history to ask a lot of questions.

Of course we have no idea who first went out and caught a

trout for fun, but it's clear that many people were doing so by the early 1700s (it should also be remembered that many colonists found *subsistence* fishing and hunting something that was fun to do at times). John Rowe, a prominent Boston businessman, kept a diary intermittently between 1764 and 1779 in which he occasionally mentioned his fishing (the diary's fishing entries were published with an introduction by John Phillips in 1929). He found excellent fishing in the ponds and brooks around Boston and Plymouth. On April 28, 1767, he fished at Duxbury Mills and "had very Good Sport. caught five Dozen Trout." The largest trout he mentions was 18 inches, a substantial size for a stream brook trout in any age.

The earliest known fly fisher (though at any time an earlier reference may be discovered) in the New World was, appropriately, a British visitor, Joseph Banks, a young naturalist who visited Labrador and Newfoundland in 1766. Banks would eventually become a leading naturalist and president of the Royal Society, but all that was before him on this trip, as he hoped to take enough specimens and do enough study to establish himself in science. Fishing historian David Ledlie recently noticed in Banks's journals (not published until 1971) that the young scholar collected his fish specimens with flies. Banks at one point wrote that the trout he caught in tidewater "offered good Diversion to an angler biting Very well at the artificial Particularly if it has gold about it. . . ." This sounds like a gold-ribbed fly of some sort.

Though the evidence is not incontrovertible, I have found probable proof of a commercial fly *tier* in Philadelphia as early as 1773, when a Quaker named Davis Hugh Davis was known to be making tackle at the George Inn.

By the early 1800s, when these fishermen began to come into clearer view for historians, they had been working the trout waters of the Eastern states for a long time, in some cases for nearly two centuries. They knew their way around, they were good at what they did, and there is no reason to doubt that they had as much fun as we do today.

But trout fishermen not only became easier for *us* to identify in the years between 1800 and 1860; they became easier for each other to see too, and thus created an important element of sporting society. The center of this movement, this growth of self-awareness and communication, was sporting publications. Trout fishing was by no means the primary subject of the largest part of these first sporting publications; horse-related sports (known as "the turf"), hunting, dogs, and other topics got more or as much attention. But trout fishermen did produce an impressive body of material that had an enormous effect on the evolution of trout fishing in America.

These earliest trout fishing journalists are unfamiliar to modern readers and have been unfairly ignored by most modern writers, who concentrate instead on the easy glamor of the later authorities and celebrities of fly-fishing. But our debt to these early writers and thinkers is considerable, and they have been neglected more out of ignorance of what they did than from any conscious decision that they did nothing important.

Though occasionally a trout-related story appeared in the scientific or popular press in the years between 1800 and 1829, it is in the latter year that we see a major development, the appearance of our first sporting periodical. *The American Turf Register and Sporting Magazine*, established by John Skinner, in Baltimore, was soon followed by the even more influential *The Spirit of the Times* in 1831, in New York. The *Spirit* was the work of William Trotter Porter, the most important figure in sporting writing before the Civil War and now universally recognized as the father of American sporting literature. Porter, through strength of personality and editorial skill, presided over the development of American sporting writing with an almost regal dignity and yet a fraternal warmth. He is one of the forgotten heroes of American trout fishing, forgotten partly because he chose to edit other writers rather than write books himself. But his guidance of other writers was wise and insightful, and he introduced American trout fishermen to practically all the major writers of the period, including British expatriate Frank Forester (the pen name of Henry William Herbert), certainly the most popular American writer on sporting subjects before 1890.

The *Spirit* and the *Turf Register* (Porter often edited both) were soon followed by other periodicals, many lasting only a few issues but all contributing to the flow of information and enthusiasm that characterizes sporting writing at any time. They accepted short reports and letters from correspondents in all parts of the country, and when that didn't fill the necessary columns, the editor himself would report on his own fishing, or turn to the British journals, sometimes shamelessly pirating material that, with slight alteration, was made to appear American in origin, other times simply reprinting it with proper credit to the original British publication. American fishermen were kept well posted on developments in British fishing in this way.

It was a strange and not easily understood period in the history of the sport, when Americans were torn between the traditions of their British forebears and their need to adjust their techniques and attitudes to the realities of American field and forest. The periodicals show a gradual transition from a near-total dependence on what had been learned on British trout streams to what we were learning on our own waters. Contrary to popular modern opinion, there is no one "birthplace" of

American fishing, be it with fly, bait, or lure. There is only this uneven, ongoing (even today), and dynamic process by which we reexamine and redefine sports that we inherited from the Old World.

Personalities and publishing history aside, what does this wealth of documentary evidence offer us, especially in answering that most important of questions, one we can ask across the generations almost as easily as we can ask it across a stream: "Whatchacatchin'emon?" The answer is pretty much the same as today: They were catchin'emon lots of things. They used flies (not always wet), they used lures (of a variety of materials, including tin and wood), and they used bait of many kinds.

I suspect that even as late as the Civil War the majority of America's trout fishermen did not buy their rods. Unless they were fly fishing and had to take a little more care to get just the right action, they probably cut themselves an appropriate pole. Some of the best early American fishing books contained detailed instructions on how to build a good fishing rod, and it was obviously much more a common practice in those days for a fisherman to build his own, even if he built a fairly fancy one, with "joints," "guides," and other hardware.

Those who did not buy their rods probably used whatever sort of cord or line was at hand, and they probably didn't bother with a reel. We have received most of our knowledge of these trout fishermen from the few of them who wrote, and those few were among the most educated and best able to afford store-bought tackle. The mass of anonymous trout fishermen of nineteenth-century America will, like their counterparts in any previous century, probably remain anonymous.

But what of the others? What did you do, for example, if you were lucky enough to live near one of New York's several tackle dealers in the 1830s or 1840s, and if you could pay the price?

You probably were accustomed to the notion that one rod was good for any kind of trout fishing. You may have owned other rods—one for trolling for lake trout, one for saltwater, perhaps another for salmon if you *really* were flush—but most of your trout fishing, whether it was with bait or fly, was done with the same rod. A good length would have been about 12 feet, maybe four sections, made of hickory or ash, with the tip section of flexible, whippy lancewood. Such a rod would seem slow and floppy to a modern fisherman, but it had its advantages. It had a great reach for poking a short leader with a hooked worm into a tight corner of a brook, and it could throw a sweet, slow roll cast with a fly line. It was also, judging from the best surviving examples, handsome and a pleasure to hold. It might have been made either in England or America, but after 1850 there was no appreciable difference in the quality of the best rods from either country, and by then it may have been that our best reels were just a tad better than theirs; at least tackle-shop promoters wanted to believe so.

In 1843, William Porter was honored by New York tackle maker John Conroy, who promoted "Porter's General Rod," a model based on Porter's personal design. With this one rod, Conroy claimed, you could do every kind of fishing. Through assembling the various alternative tips and other sections, it could become a light trout rod or a "heavy, powerful rod, sufficiently strong to play a thirty-pound salmon." It was apparently quite popular, though by the end of the century the idea of the general rod was no longer fashionable and was even ridiculed.

Hooks were almost always attached to the line by a snell, the hook bound permanently to a short gut or hair leader. Snelled flies (the leader was tied onto the hook before the fly was tied) ruled fly-fishing until well after 1900 in many parts of the country.

Baits were, as they are now, as numerous as the items in the trout's diet. Worms seem to be mentioned most of all, though minnows were popular too. You used what you could get, and if the published reports are any indication, bait was all you really needed to catch a lot of trout.

There was no shortage of innovation and experimentation. Porter, writing in the *Turf Register* in September of 1840, about fishing in the Adirondacks, described a rig for lake trout fishing that must have strained even his substantial creative resources:

> In trolling, we made our leader fourteen feet long, the precise length of our rod, using one of Conroy's patent reels containing three hundred feet of braided-silk line, strong enough to hold a 3 yr. old colt. At the end of our leader we had a set of snap-hooks, with a second set four feet above it, on each of which we played a live minnow, very much to our satisfaction, however they may have enjoyed it. Above the snaps at equal distances we looped on five large salmon flies. The whole arrangement made something of a display, as we thought, and the trout must also have been "mightily taken with it," for we took two or three at a time!

Something of a display indeed. Even admitting that he was after 30-pound lake trout, the gear seems a bit heavy, even if he was kidding about the three-year-old colt.

Flies were as much a matter of personal taste as they are

now. Many of the early authors (Forester and Brown among them) simply parroted the lists of flies in British books, but some writers were already coming up with patterns of their own. George Washington Bethune, in his notes to the first American edition of Walton's *Compleat Angler* (1847), made it clear that several of his angling colleagues were experimenting, not only with British patterns but with their own variations and originals, on waters from New Jersey to the Adirondacks. American fly fishers were well on their way to developing their own approaches to imitation by the end of the Civil War.

American trout fishermen seem always to have been wanderers. Even the first exploring parties into some regions, such as the Lewis and Clark expedition, were taking trout if only to eat or preserve as study specimens. But the vast American wilderness beckoned irresistibly to generations of trout fishers so irresistibly that many waters were fished surprisingly early. Of course the coastal streams were explored first, and those nearest inland settlements. But by the 1840s sportsmen had found their way into the immense Adirondack region and were already well established along the shores of New England lakes and streams. A few recent adventurers were reporting outstanding fishing in the Catskills and the Poconos, and others were working their way farther west in Pennsylvania. A few fishermen had discovered (and with unusual discretion, not publicized) the monumental trout of Maine's Rangeley region, and others were starting to fill in the many gaps in the trout-fishing map here and there—Vermont, Virginia, New York, Pennsylvania, wherever trout waters could be found.

From those Eastern outposts came the great leaps. In this respect at least, Blakey was right: American fishermen carried their fly rods into the most remote wilderness areas even before the Civil War. By the 1850s, reports were coming in to the sporting periodicals of incredible trout fishing in California, Oregon, and Washington. In 1860, a naturalist listing the fauna of Montana Territory in a scientific journal commented incidentally that in that year soldiers were fishing for cutthroat trout, using both bait and flies. Ten years later even the exploration-resistant Yellowstone plateau had been fished with flies. A three- or four-piece trout rod in a protective frame is light and not hard to carry, and a few sharp hooks are a good hedge against hunger in wild country; no wonder so many streams and lakes were fished so soon.

But the explorer and settler was often accompanied or even preceded by the sportsman, and sometimes all three were in one body, so that a man seeking a pass over a mountain range may also have been a farmer seeking a cabin site and a trout enthusiast looking for a rise. It must have been enormously exciting, knowing one could find so many things at once: new country, a new home, and unfished waters.

Different waters demand different tactics, so that sportsmen in each region, indeed on each stream and pond, were influenced by local conditions. It has been this collection of challenges that has brought us so much in the way of tackle evolution, new techniques, and even philosophical growth, for trout fishermen, like other sportsmen, are products of their environment. As we influence the trout and its environment, so does that environment influence us. We are very lucky, in fact, that there *is* no single birthplace of our tradition; if there were it would be a far less vital sport.

There is more to fishing than the tackle and the techniques, no matter how varied and colorful those may be. There is the complex intellectual baggage we carry along just as we carry our rods and our creels. There are the things we believe are right, or sporting, and there are the things we believe are important about the experience. It is this less tangible part of the trout-fishing experience that explains why we read Robert Traver or Nick Lyons as avidly as we read Doug Swisher and Carl Richards or Gary LaFontaine. We long to know more than "how," and part of what we want to know is "why."

That is nothing new. Just as these early anglers debated which rods, flies, baits, and reels were best, they debated many other things. I find it especially apropos to modern trout fishing that they were like us in their prejudices. Listen to these voices from 150 years ago and see if anything has changed. First, the grand old man himself, William Trotter Porter:

> Fly fishing has been designated the royal and aristocratic branch of the angler's craft, and unquestionably it is the most difficult, the most elegant, and to men of taste, by myriads of degrees the most exciting and pleasant mode of angling.

Then try Chandler Gilman, from his book *Life on the Lakes* (1836):

> Trolling! that vile, that murderous practice! abhorred at once and despised by all good men and true anglers. He permit it or countenance it? Never. The bones of old Isaac Walton would move in his coffin in horror at the degeneration of his disciple!

Then from an 1832 correspondent from New Hampshire, writing to the *Turf Register* to complain that British flies were worthless for "catching Yankee trout":

I soon ascertained that the patent English line and *artificial fly* would not do. Our fish are too Republican, or too shrewd, or too stupid, to understand the *science of English* trout fishing. I therefore took the common hook and worm, with a simple line and light sinker, and a rod cut on the spot; they then understood, and we readily caught in a short time, twenty-three fine *brook Trout.*

These sorts of gibes—some gentle, some mean, some deeply bigoted—appeared occasionally in the published conversations of anglers then as they do now. The process by which we define good sportsmanship is a never-ending one. We will always differ with each other, to say nothing of with fishermen in other countries (however much we may lose touch with modern British fishing, we will probably never stop invoking Walton's name on behalf of our favorite argument), over what's right and proper in trout fishing. When it comes to a tolerance for the opinions and ideas of other fishermen, I can't say that we're all that much advanced over the trout fishermen of 150 years ago. But then, after all, we're only trout fishermen; what do I expect?

And yet after all my reading in early American trout fishing, I find it immensely attractive. Knowing I cannot fish back then is not a problem; I don't really need to. But at the same time I do want to know what it was like. I want to know not just so I can better understand how our sport evolved, though that does intrigue me, and not out of some arid antiquarian interest in old ways, but because fishing is a shared experience and I can share these great old fishing trips vicariously and quite pleasurably. What must it have been like, for example, to kill, as one *Turf Register* correspondent reported, 570 trout in one day on a Vermont stream, and to do so at a time when there was often no guilt attached to the activity? Well, according to the correspondent, it was sport better even than that "known to Izaak Walton of old, that prince of anglers; and such as few of us will ever have the opportunity of knowing again." True enough, if only because you can only do that to a stream once in a great while and still expect to find any trout in it at all.

But there's no more point in resenting that foolish, greedy fisherman than there is in envying him; it's just that what he did is interesting to me. There is something to be shared in a fishing story, even if it's told in archaic language, and it's the same thing we share when we read the modern books and magazines or swap tales with our friends. We trout fishermen have a sort of race memory in our written and oral traditions, so we can enjoy the triumphs and shake our heads over the disasters of fishing trips long ago just as we do when our neighbor tells us his latest fishing story. Knowing more about early American trout fishing only allows me to stretch that connection back further, gives me even more stories to remember and more dreams to share.

Four

CARLISLE MORNINGS

A T FIRST glance, southeastern Pennsylvania's Letort Spring Run may seem smaller than it should; a visiting fly fisherman might object that surely the stream that inspired the works of some of America's most thoughtful and innovative fly-fishing writers must be bigger than *this*. Many fishermen probably subconsciously imagine the Letort as a river, rather than take "spring run" at face value. As well, the idyllic photos in Vincent Marinaro's fly-fishing classic, *A Modern Dry Fly Code* (1950), the most enduring and powerfully written book inspired by the Letort, show only a few stretches of water where the stream broadens out in spacious, willow-lined meadows.

But that is only the first of the shocks the visitor may re-

ceive, followed quickly by the realization that at least some of
those roomy stretches Marinaro photographed are now under
pavement, townhouses, and turnpike bridges. The town of
Carlisle, through which the creek flows, has lined much of the
stream with the sprawl of a growing community, and present-
day fishermen spend an inordinate amount of time trying to
guard the water against more damage.

The next shock, for me at least, was the realization that the
Letort was not alone. I was aware of a few of the other more
notable of the area's little trout streams, but it wasn't until I
drove the streets of the nearby towns and the county highways
that my spring-creek search image began to kick in. A small
brook would pass under the road, and I'd catch a quick glimpse
of long, trailing weeds in the water, and I'd ask whatever local I
was riding with, "Whatwazzat?" This part of Pennsylvania, and
indeed south into Maryland, must once have been a lacework
of great trout streams—and could be again if only we weren't
so busy doing other things with the land.

Despite all the obvious degradations and intrusions, if the
visitor is any kind of fisherman at all, the changes won't stop
him or her from feeling the Letort's quiet magic. It is still possible to find a sheltered bend or a more rural reach of water,
where the humming of the traffic is muffled and the only build-
ings in sight are the grand old limestone farmhouses that
graced the setting in Marinaro's day. And fishing the stream,
either alone or with some of the local veterans, it becomes easy
to understand why this little river and its wonderful sister
streams, known locally as the "limestoners," have been such
powerful molders of fishermen.

Though it has only been in the past half century that the
Letort has won fame for its difficult trout and its great writers,
the stream has had an important role in American fly-fishing

for at least four times that long, giving it a continuous history of fly-fishing longer than virtually any other American trout stream, including the celebrated Catskill streams that many people still incorrectly consider the "birthplace" of fly-fishing in the New World. Most residents of the Carlisle area, fishermen or not, have no idea how much this modest little stream has meant to the development of the sport.

Written record of the stream goes back well beyond two centuries ago. Reverend Conway Wing's grand and absorbing *History of Cumberland County, Pennsylvania* (1879) quotes a letter from John O'Neal to Governor James Hamilton, written on May 27, 1753, from the newly established town of Carlisle, which had only five "dwelling houses" at that date:

> The situation, however, is handsome, in the centre of a valley, with a mountain bounding it on the north and the south, at a distance of seven miles. The wood consists principally of oak and hickory. The limestone will be of great advantage to the future settlers, being in abundance. A limekiln stands on the centre square, near what is called the deep quarry, from which is obtained good building stone. A large stream of water runs about two miles from the village, which may at a future period, be rendered navigable. A fine spring flows to the east, called Le Tort, after the Indian interpreter who settled on its head about the year 1720.

There is much of importance to fishermen in this straightforward description. James Le Tort (also spelled Le Tart but eventually standardized as Letort) was by most accounts the first white person to settle in present-day Cumberland County, building a cabin there. He traded with the local Native Americans (who at one point apparently burned the cabin, whatever that tells us about Le Tort the trader) and eventually became an interpreter, though little seems known about his other activities between 1720 and the 1750s.

More important than the stream's namesake is its character, which is also hinted at in this letter. The "large stream of water" 2 miles from the village must be the Conodoguinet, itself a fine fishing stream of which I will have more to say later in this book. The Letort empties into the Conodoguinet northeast of Carlisle, heightening the complexity of the local stream ecology as the cold waters of the little trout stream blend with the warm lowland flow of the larger river.

But the most important feature of the Letort's valley is revealed in O'Neal's mentions of limestone. Limestone builds much more than sturdy barns and beautiful homes; it builds big trout. The streams issuing from the limestone "springs" are enriched by calcium carbonate, creating an extremely hospitable environment for aquatic vegetation (watercress is a great sign of a limestone stream), which in turn serves both to oxygenate the water and to host robust populations of aquatic insects and other invertebrates that trout feed on.

Then too, streams born in limestone country are the product of large subterranean aquifers not readily affected by short-term changes in climate conditions. While the typical mountain stream, with its steep gradient and its sources in rain and melting snow, experiences all manner of temperature variation, flood, and drought, the limestoners run clear, stable, and steady unless humans tinker too much with the whole watershed (something that has happened too often to the Letort and the others in recent decades). Of course this stability just makes life that much easier for the fish, who spend no time dodging trees ripped loose in floods, or dealing with a host of other environmental shocks, from anchor ice in winter to overheated water during summer droughts. A healthy limestoner is one of nature's great fish factories; wherever I have fished a spring, creek, from the Cascades to the Appalachians to the many famous and anonymous ones in my general neighborhood near Yellowstone, I have recognized the type and wished we had a good National Spring Creek Protection Act so that these precious little aquatic ecosystems could have the kind of care they deserve. They are home to such a rich diversity of life, in their currents and well back from their banks, that they are often a kind of oasis for plant and animal species that would be lost to the area without them. Of course it doesn't hurt at all, in my enthusiasm for these places, that among their most well-nurtured species are trout.

What modern fly fishermen learn from the Letort and the other limestoners, though, is that lots of fish don't directly equate with lots of fish *caught*. All the conditions that make life so easy for the fish also make them finicky feeders, and a trout in a slow-flowing, tricky-currented pool, with plenty of leisure to inspect the passing smorgasbord of mayflies, ants, cressbugs, and artificial flies, is a trout that will send a lot of modern fishermen home mumbling to themselves. The Letort doesn't just grow big trout; it grows discriminating trout.

It was exactly that combination of qualities that made it "great" in the peculiar lexicon of anglers. The best fishing, at least for the most thoughtful fly fishermen, has usually been the most challenging fishing—the fishing that made you think and work the hardest and learn the most. So the Letort, besides being a trout factory, has also become an idea factory, where new fly patterns and techniques were tested and improved. As I said, over the past fifty years or so, this has resulted in a series of books by writers whose thinking was largely shaped by this little stream. Local fishermen intone the names of local masters—Marinaro, Fox, Koch, Shenk, and so on—the way baseball fans speak in awe of great pitchers and hitters.

Probably because of the photographs taken of nineteenth-century anglers in their ties and bowler hats, staring with grim formality during the long exposure required, earlier generations of American fishermen are often thought of as stiff, dull, and a little sappy. But these earlier generations of fishermen were a lively, thoughtful crowd, a diverse bunch of right- and wrong-minded characters, some jolly, some serious, some silly, and all just as obsessed with fishing as we are. One of the most intriguing of them all grew up within casting distance of the great Pennsylvania limestoners.

His name was George Gibson, and he was born in Pennsylvania about 1775. Like his father, he had a successful career in the U.S. Army, rising to the rank of major general; at the time of his death, in 1861, he was called "one of the patriarchs of the army." A friend of Winfield Scott, Andrew Jackson (who reportedly wanted to name him to the Supreme Court, but never had the opportunity), and many other prominent citizens, Gibson was too busy for many extended fishing and hunting trips, but he performed a rare service for history by writing, between 1829 and 1849, a series of spirited little notes and articles about hunting and fishing for the sporting press, especially *The American Turf Register* and *The Spirit of the Times*. These make him one of America's very first fishing writers, and reveal him not only as a creative angler but also as the kind of guy you'd like to have along on your next trip.

According to his published statements (and I'm still in

search of unpublished material), he started fishing around 1790 or so and seems to have made annual trips from Washington back to Carlisle to fish the limestone streams, especially the Letort (which he spelled "Letart") and Big Spring, even during the busiest times of his career.

What is engaging about Gibson is how he thought, and how he dealt with problems and issues we still face today. Reading about his little adventures, and thinking about his opinions, is fun because we fishermen today can usually sympathize with what he was up against. Because of that, and because he deserves the attention anyway, I want to give him plenty of room to talk here. I am introducing you to a truly lost fishing expert, with an intelligent and clever voice that deserves to be heard again.

American Turf Register editor William Porter contacted Gibson in 1829 and asked him to describe his local fishing. Here is the answer, published in September of that year. This letter was perhaps the earliest firsthand "article" about local trout-fishing experiences to appear in an American magazine (there were earlier articles, but they are less personal and specific and may have been mostly plagiarized from British publications):

> *Sir*,—You ask me for a paper on trout and trout fishing in Pennsylvania. This you shall have with pleasure, but as I am not more than a *practical* man in such matters, you cannot expect much.
>
> Although I commenced *wetting* flies in times long gone by, my experience extends only to Cumberland county; but trout were formerly found in all the limestone springs in the state. Owing, however, to the villainous practice of netting them, they are extinct in some streams, and scarce in others.
>
> In Cumberland, there are three good trout streams. Big

Spring, west of Carlisle, runs a distance of five miles, and turns six flouring mills, and affords fine sport almost the whole distance. A law of the state makes it penal to net in this stream, and forbids the taking of trout between the months of July and April. It is the only spring branch in the state protected by law; the good effects of which is so apparent, that it is hoped other streams will receive the like protection.

The Letart which flows past Carlisle, is another good stream. It runs about four miles through meadow grounds, and turns three flouring mills. It formerly afforded excellent sport, but owing to the infamous practice of *netting* and setting *night lines*, the fish have been much lessened in numbers and size.

Silver-spring, east and north of Carlisle, runs half a mile, and turns two flouring mills. This stream breeds the largest and best trout of any in the state—they are from one to three pounds, and it requires nice tackle and an experienced hand to land them.

The rod used is fifteen or sixteen feet long, very delicate, and throws from twenty to thirty feet of line—and in all these streams the fisherman is most successful with the artificial fly. The colour used in April is black or dark brown; in May, dun or red hackle; in June and July, imitations of the miller's or candle flies are found best.

The habits of this fish is soon told. In winter they seek the deep calm pool, and seldom or never change their position or go abroad. In spring and summer, they delight in rapids. They feed on flies, worms, water snails, and prey on small fish. They spawn in September, and for that purpose select ripples and shoal water, with gravel and sandy bottom. When the spawn or young trout is brought out, it approaches close to the shore, or gets into very shoal water to protect it from the larger fish, for it is a fact that the large trout will kill and eat the small ones. As he gains strength and size he returns to deep water, and in time becomes the monarch of his pool.

In conclusion, I will give you my first evening at Silver-spring. It was long since, with a party of five, and all bait fishers except myself. The proprietor of the grounds advised me to take bait. He had never been successful with a fly. I would not be advised. The evening was fine—a cloud obscured the sun, a gentle breeze rippled the pool, and such was my success, that in less than one hour, I landed twenty trout, from one to two pounds each. The proprietor cried "enough."—I asked for the privilege of another cast. I made one, and hooked a large trout with my bobbing fly, and in playing him, another of equal size ran at and was hooked by my trail fly, and both were landed in handsome style. The last throw was fatal to my sports in that pool—for I never after was a welcome visitor, but many is the day I have met with nearly as good success in the other mill pool.

This information-rich tale, with its appreciation for natural history as well as for sport, is about as good a summary as Porter could possibly have hoped for and almost all we could want today too. We learn, for example, that even 170 years ago, trout had too many human enemies; the "villainous practice of netting" had pretty much cleaned out some streams, and regulations of any sort were only in effect on one of these wonderful streams. Studying Gibson's trout fishing is a poor exercise in nostalgia for the good old days; often they weren't all that good.

As important, we learn a lot about tackle, which was certainly different from that carried by Letort regulars today. A 15-foot-long fly rod seems absurd to most modern fly fishermen, who would find that Gibson's description of it as "very

delicate" really meant "floppy." Most modern fly fishermen use
rods less than 9 feet long, and many on the Letort prefer rods
less than 7 feet. But casting was a slow, soft, and often quite effective process with this outfit. I can see the advantages of such
a rig, if I could keep it and my errant back casts out of the trees.
On those little streams, with their narrow, winding channels of
water moving between the weed beds, 15 feet of rod could give
me quite a reach and better line control than I have now, and
that would force me to make far fewer and certainly much gen-
tler casts than the quick and sometimes too spashly ones I
make with a fast graphite rod. Anyway, I'd like to try it (hoping
all the while that the Letort's foremost short-rod advocate, Ed
Shenk, would forgive me).

Gibson's fly terminology might be a little obscure, so I'll explain that he was using a two-fly "cast," with a "tail fly" (or, as
he called it, a "trail fly") on the very end of the line and a
"bob" fly (what he called a "bobbing fly") tied on a short section of leader a foot or two up from the tail fly. Multiple-fly
casts were very common in his time and have remained popular for much of the time since with wet-fly fishermen. His fly
line was probably horsehair or some combination of horsehair
and other fibers, and his leader was gut. Flies were typically
tied with a short snell of gut under the body; the snell, a few
inches long at most, had a loop on its end, by which it was attached to the rest of the leader. It sounds as if Gibson didn't
bother with a reel, but just tied his fly line to the rod. Being a
fairly well-off man, he probably had a store-bought rod, with a
wire loop at the tip, so that he could retrieve or lengthen line
as need be.

But what most attracts me to Gibson are his discussions of
fly patterns. Like many thoughtful fishermen, he seemed interested in the development of flies for the particular waters he

fished, rather than standard fly patterns purchased in some sporting goods shop. Thousands of fly patterns have been developed over the past five centuries of fly-fishing, many of which were intended to imitate a certain mayfly or other invertebrate fish feed on. This process of "matching the hatch" has gone on everywhere trout rise and fishermen cast, so it's safe to assume Gibson and his friends participated in it.

From the very simple selection of flies Gibson described in this first letter, he went on in other letters to give us quite a few patterns, certainly some of the first records we have of fly patterns used on American waters. In several of his later letters, he discussed the success of this or that pattern under different circumstances. In June 1830, he reported that on his "first visit to Big spring, a dun wing over a red heckle, was a killing fly; but in a few days after, at the same place, not a trout would rise at it," and further related that in adjoining pools on Silver Spring, two completely different flies—a miller (a mothlike fly) and a peacock-bodied, brown-winged fly—were required. On the Letort, "a small grey fly was at all times in season." It's a little frustrating, trying to figure out how he chose these patterns. He never came right out and said he picked up some living insects, looked at them, and rooted through his fly book for a good match, but in this same letter he did allow that "I have been particular in noting the colour of my flies, and the frequent changes necessary for the benefit of young sportsmen; they but too often stick to the same fly, and the same spot of ground, when they ought to change both."

Whether he bothered with stream entomology or not, Gibson obviously spent a fair amount of time wondering about flies himself. He had little use for the old British theory of a single specific fly for every month:

It is nonsense to believe there is a colour for every month—
it is not so—for in fishing three mill pools on the same stream
on the same day, I have found, that to be successful, I had to
change my fly and the colour of it at each pool; and in fishing
in the same places a few days after, the only fly trout would rise
to, was a small grey one, and to such a one they would rise
freely in all the pools. In the early part of the season when the
trout is poor, he will run at anything; but towards June he becomes a perfect epicure in his feeding at such time.

North America's native trout, including the brook trout of
the East and the cutthroat and rainbows of the West, have reputations for being easily caught compared to Old World brown
trout. Informal tests of catch rates suggest that the cutthroat
may be even more gullible than the brookie, but all these
species can also be nearly uncatchable in some circumstances.
The places they are most difficult are usually similar to the
limestoners: slow currents, low, clear water, and abundant
food, with lots of time for the fish to inspect each offering. I
have encountered brook trout on the late-summer Battenkill,
and cutthroats on the spring creeks of Jackson Hole, that were
as canny and selective as any brown I've seen, and it appears
that Gibson ran into the same situation with his local native
brook trout. He observed, as would generations of later fishermen, that his "limped [*sic*] lime-stone brooks" required more
careful attention to fly pattern than might be necessary elsewhere. That glassy water surface hides many tiny vagrant
currents and eddies that cause an artificial fly to "drag" unnatu-
rally across the flow rather than drift with it; trout have a dia-
bolical ability to notice these little things. Gibson understood
that the streams were special, whether or not he knew what

made them that way. Writing in *The American Turf Register* in June 1838, he reported on the challenge of catching fish in such places:

> I was once at Big Spring, in Cumberland Co. Pennsylvania, with a young friend from New York who said his flies were of the right sort. We commenced fishing near each other. Very soon I landed four or six brace [a brace is a pair], but not a trout would rise to his fly. I examined it, and found it a peacock body and peacock wing. I took a small grey fly from my own book and tied it on his hooks, and had the pleasure of seeing him kill fifteen brace with it. Another time I was at Silver Spring, in the same county. It was an evening of alternate clouds and sunshine, with a gentle breeze, and exactly what fly-fishers call a killing day; yet for one hour, not a trout would rise, although I changed my fly several times.—At last I tried a light rust-colored body and a long dark wing, and marked "Irish Salmon," and with that fly I killed, without changing the spot on which I stood, fourteen trout weighing from two to two and a half pounds each. All I contend for, is, that much of our success in fishing depends on the size and colour of our flies, and the firmness of the gut or sinew next the fly.

Again, Gibson doesn't tell us if he changed flies in order to better match some natural insect, or just as a matter of habit, to try something different (a fly marked Irish Salmon, I assume, was a store-bought pattern with a label on it, and being a salmon fly was probably fairly large). In other letters he repeated this position; one must adapt one's flies, both in color and size, to the waters.

There is little talk of variation in fly "style." That is, he gives little hint of flies with different shapes or proportions; his mention of the Irish Salmon fly having a "long" wing is a rare case of him distinguishing the shape of one fly from another. From this we might assume that his flies were all pretty much the same proportion, with only the colors and materials changing, or that he just didn't bother to tell us about anything so detailed. But in one case, one of fortuitous circumstances that could lead to new insights, fly style became very important:

> I will relate what happened to me when whipping for trout at Irvine's Pond on Big Spring a few years since. I was casting a drab fly but did not land many fish. In taking my hook from the fourth or fifth trout, I discovered that nothing remained of the fly but the mohair body, and that somewhat worn. I thought it strange that I could take a fine fish with such a nondescript fly, so unlike any thing I had ever seen. I tried it again, and such was my success that Mr. Caruthers left his stand and came up to look at my fly. I clipped the wings from one like that on my line and gave it to him, and with those two flies we took about fifty brace of trout. These nondescript flies were preserved and imitated, and we tried them again at the same place after a lapse of only a few days, but not a fish would touch them. In the elegant collection of flies presented to me by Sir Charles Vaughn after his return to England, there were several sorts of flies unlike any insect seen in this country, and yet I have taken trout with them, but it was in swift rapid water.

There is so much here to wonder about. Did the wingless flies accidentally imitate some nymph or emerging insect? Gibson never says much about his actual fishing techniques on these still millponds, so we don't know how deeply he allowed the flies to sink (if they sank at all; from some of his descriptions it's obvious that at times he fished on or right under the surface), or what motion he gave them as he retrieved them. The damaged fly that keeps working is a persistent minor theme in fishing lore, though; for some reason, beat-up flies often do well, and it could be that the fish, through their chewing, inadvertently turn a so-so pattern into a good imitation of something they were interested in just then.

But as much wonder can be invested in figuring out how Gibson's flies equate with modern insect hatches on these streams. His flies with "bodies of dirty yellowish white or bright yellow" could easily be intentional imitations of the family of small yellow mayflies modern fishermen call sulfurs, so common at dusk on the streams of the Cumberland Valley. But until more evidence turns up (like maybe a fishing diary, or even an old fly book from that period), we can't really know because we can't tell exactly how they tied these flies. In the meantime, it would be worth the time of some enterprising limestone regular to compile a list of Gibson's patterns and the times at which he reported them successful and try to determine what hatches they might have been imitating.

So what was a day of fishing like for George Gibson? In some ways it was much different from today's outings; remember that he told of taking "fifty brace" (one hundred) trout in a day. That would be an extraordinary catch today (as well as illegal), but seems to have happened now and then in his day. He fished without the rush and tumult of modern freeway traffic in the distance, but without the ease of automobile transportation to any stretch of the stream he might like. He fished with tackle most modern fishermen would find clumsy and slow, but that was beautifully made, masterfully handled, and demonstrably effective. He fished without the modern hordes of experts and beginners for company, but also without the protection their united power gave the stream from further degradation.

Maybe the most important thing Gibson tells us in his little letters is that he wasn't alone. He described many fishing companions, making it clear that fly-fishing was a long-established and honored use of the stream, practiced by a sizeable brotherhood of sportsmen (he never mentions women). Then, as now, fly-fishing was a fairly social sport, with sportsmen banding together for fishing, arguing, and everything else to do with good company, including the recognition of their greatest champions; in his day, as in ours, there were those rare souls so expert that they seemed almost superhuman. In 1830, Gibson wrote the following about an admired fishing companion, whom he described as "one of the best fly fishers of the age":

> Jo makes his own lines and flies, holds a rod eighteen feet long, and throws thirty-six or forty feet of line with one hand, and no amateur can avoid a bush, flank an eddy, or drop into a ripple with more certainty or more ease. And there is one trait in his character decidedly sportsman-[like]—*he never sold a trout in his life* . . .

It is in remarks like these that Gibson fully reveals how much like us he was. He participated in the very same quest we do today, with all its philosophical wranglings, technical distractions, and social amenities, and he detested all the threats to his beloved trout, whether pollution, or netting or other commercial fishing.

And for all the changes the Letort has experienced—the replacement of the native fish with browns and rainbows, the increasing crowds, the wholesale industrial development of so much of the watershed, the many advances in tackle and techniques—the actual fishing couldn't have been much different from today. The Letort is in a lovely setting, lovelier then, without all the recent construction, but lovely in any age just because its quiet, weed-draped currents run through beautiful country that even the most hideous development can't entirely ruin.

No doubt the morning meadows were strung with as many spiderwebs and just as thick with nettles. No doubt the sun was hot even early in the day, and I suppose July was just as muggy and sticky then as it is now. Gibson's clothes were probably damp with dew and perspiration by the time he reached the water. The lush, rank vegetation of the trail must have caught at him as he passed. A 15-foot rod must have been a real nuisance to carry; the line would snag on trees and brush, making the old fisherman stumble and cuss.

But when he reached the water, and the cold currents soaked his leggings, and the cooler air above the stream hit the perspiration on his forehead, and the 2-pounders began to rise within range of that long, gentle fly rod, the Letort's magic must have taken hold just as it does now, and for a little while everything else was forgotten.

Five

BATTENKILL SUMMERS

I N 1 9 7 7, after spending the better part of six years devoted to Yellowstone and its wonders, I was growing restless. It seemed that the good I could do as a seasonal employee in the park was limited, and I had reached that destructive but universally fashionable state where you begin to see your bosses—decent, bright people who had their own ambitions and sense of direction—as obstacles. I was ready for a change, and perhaps the greatest sign of that was that I had lost some of my interest in fishing and become more absorbed in my history studies.

By now I had become a voracious reader of fishing books and had already made a list of other good trout country I would like to live in, a list that included New England. Though I knew I'd eventually return to Yellowstone, I also knew it was time to do something else, so it was a matter of great excitement and unbelievable good fortune that late that year I was offered a job as the first full-time executive director of what was then called the Museum of American Fly Fishing (it was later renamed the American Museum of Fly Fishing, and I'm still convinced there are at least five living people, me included, who understand and appreciate the distinction between the two names).

Executive director was a title of considerably more pomp than circumstance. The museum, founded in the late 1960s as the idea of *Field & Stream* art director Hermann Kessler and maintained almost solely through the generosity of the Perkins family of the Orvis company, had survived and even flourished with largely volunteer help, thanks to the high energy and quality of the volunteers. But they would have been the first to point out that it had a long way to go to become a real, professional museum, just as I had a long way to go to become a real, professional museum director.

However big a step hiring a director may have been for the museum, it was an absolutely enormous one for me. When I loaded up my Super Beetle and left Yellowstone that November, I had only the vaguest idea of what I would do when I reached Manchester, Vermont. It was an exciting time, and an almost ideal position for me. I was just old enough to have accumulated at least a little background in the variety of professional fields that museum work involves—exhibit planning and design, editing, public speaking, writing, and the like— and I had been an avid fly fisherman and student of fishing history just long enough to know how intriguing it could be.

The next five years were really busy, and my learning curve must have been nearly vertical the whole time. With the help of a batch of new friends, I saw to the creation of all new exhibits, overhauled the magazine that the museum published, launched a banquet-auction program to raise money, tried to increase membership, oversaw the acquisition of hundreds of new objects of extraordinary value to the collection, and tended to all the administrative details accompanying the running of even the smallest of institutions. I never seemed to do anything really well, but I made enough happen to please my officers and trustees.

At the same time, I soaked up huge amounts of gloriously disorganized information and impressions about fly-fishing. I saw the flies of the best tiers in American history, waggled classic fly rods by the score, talked to good fishermen beyond counting, read books I had never even hoped to see, and got an inside look at the industry behind fly-fishing. It was like taking a five-year college course in what fly-fishing was all about, taught by the best authorities. No, it wasn't *like* that; it *was* that. It was better for me than I could have imagined, and in many ways, not at all what I'd expected.

My Western friends had warned me that living in the East would be a real challenge for me, because everyone knew that there were huge crowds of people with the manners of Californians, it was impossible to get a good steak, and the rivers were all fished out. This sort of talk didn't prepare me for the real problem. The people I met in Vermont were as varied, wonderful, and awful as people everywhere else, including California. I couldn't afford steak. And the river seemed to have a lot of fish in it. I just couldn't catch them.

At the time, long before the museum acquired its own building in Manchester, the public exhibits were in rented space in the Orvis store, and my office was in an old Orvis warehouse about half a mile away, on Union Street, just down from the

Equinox Hotel in the spectacularly picturesque historic district of the old village. After work I'd drive down the hill to a grassy-banked stretch of the Battenkill (or Batten Kill). There for a couple of hours I would indulge my quixotic impulse to try to catch at least one of the river's bewilderingly uncooperative fish. Yellowstone was rarely like this.

Sometimes I would work my way upstream, where the trees closed over the water like a tunnel, and brush and fenceposts reached out to grab my undisciplined back casts. As dusk deepened, a low fog would drift into the tunnel. If I was concentrating hard, I wouldn't notice the fog until I was more or less in it, a misty blanket that seemed almost to glow until I looked around and tried to find the source of the light but couldn't. Though the catching didn't improve in this ethereal setting, the fishing became an intimate thing, a celebration of solitude in a very small space. The river and the looming trees faded to gray only a few yards in all directions, and even the current's noise was muted. Every so often, a small trout would embarrass itself and take my dry fly, but more often I had to settle for the happy satisfactions of making an occasional good cast to a difficult spot, knowing that any fish other than a Battenkill trout would have taken such a fine delivery with confidence.

Southwestern Vermont is dominated, geographically at least, by something the geologists call the Vermont Valley. It is a long, narrow trough that runs north and south between the Green Mountains (the Green Mountain Massif, if you prefer) to the east and the Taconics (The Taconic klippe, formally) to the west. Both mountain ranges are almost completely covered with mixed forests, supporting a rich variety of wildlife.

The seasons were often displayed on the mountainsides with

textbook clarity. I recall a late autumn day when the valley, with its small, white-homed villages, rolling golf courses, and scattered patches of forest, was still in a deep summer green, while the lower slopes were blazing with New England's famous fall colors and the very highest ridges were all but bare of trees and dusted in new snow.

The Battenkill spends the first 15 or so miles of its life flowing south, down the Vermont Valley. Mad Tom Brook tumbled out of a narrow little draw in Green Mountain National Forest just across the valley from my cottage in East Dorset, and I often walked along it and the Battenkill, which it joined right there, for the company of rising trout and the occasional sight of bobolinks, orioles, and, on a banner day, a pair of Virginia rails. Here, everything alive in the water seemed small and quick, as in hundreds of other small Eastern mountain streams. There was little at the upper end of the river to suggest that the Battenkill would soon turn into anything unusual, much less into the singular river it is.

It moves more or less due south from East Dorset for 5 miles, to Manchester, where it is joined by the West Branch, then continues on through narrow farms, receiving any number of smaller streams, including Bourn Brook from the east and Munson's Brook from the west, and, a couple miles downstream from Manchester, Lye Brook, coming out of the Lye Brook Wilderness Area in Green Mountain National Forest. When the museum was first launched, the famous painter and angler Ogden Pleissner donated a portion of the print run of *Lye Brook Pool*, his painting of the confluence of the brook and the river, for fund-raising purposes.

Much of the river is densely forested on both banks—one stretch below Manchester is known locally as "the jungle"—so that while walking its banks, you often have little idea how near you are to settled country. Along most of the river, the development is limited to farmhouses, barns, and the occasional small village, though the outlet malls have multiplied ominously in recent years. I had no trouble finding sufficiently bucolic settings for my fishing.

After passing Sunderland and receiving the waters of the Roaring Branch from the east, the river arrives at Arlington, makes a right turn along Route 313, and heads west toward the New York border. The lower river in Vermont, the last 10 miles or so, seems perhaps the most Norman Rockwellian stretch of this calendar-grade watershed, possibly because Rockwell lived here for many years, frequently painting people and places (one of the most appealing being the red covered bridge across the river below Arlington, near his former home). These last few Vermont miles also seemed to me to be the most popular for fishermen, as the river is of good size and easily wadable, with plenty of deep stretches holding larger fish. The New York Battenkill is also a fine trout stream, with its own rich lore and natural history, and I did fish it some, especially late in the year, after the Vermont water was closed, but I rarely needed to go that far, and somehow going over there made me feel a little too close to New York City.

There is little agreement on how the river got its name. One historian argued that "Batten" was probably the surname of some forgotten settler or visitor, another was confident that the name originated as a distortion of the name of Bartholomew Van Hogeboom, a pioneer in Stillwater, New York. According to latter theory, "Bart's Kill" became Battenkill over time. Several recent writers have referred to an 1868 edition of *Vermont Historical Magazine*, which said that Battenkill was Dutch for "fertilizing stream." Perhaps the most satisfying alternative name is Ondawa, which in Mohawk meant "white stream," and which was still in common usage among local residents in the late 1800s. The trick, whether you spell it Battenkill or Batten Kill, is to let it go at that, and not add "river." "Kill" is Dutch for river, so Battenkill River is redundant.

When I moved to Vermont from Yellowstone, where you could walk for miles through forests with no sign of human presence, it was quite a shock; it seemed that whatever steep forested hillside I scrambled up, I suddenly came upon a crumbling stone wall, or an old foundation, or a forgotten apple orchard. Manchester, the town most associated with the river (at least as far as its fame beyond the state goes) was incorporated in 1761 and by 1830 had a population of 1,525 already engaged in a massive alteration of the landscape. Huge tracts of forest were clearcut for farms; by 1850, three-quarters of Vermont's once-continuous forests were gone, and the state was reduced to what historian Charles Johnson called a "biological wasteland." Though landscape ecology isn't quite as simple as Johnson's view implies, it was certain that the wholesale timber harvest had disastrous effects on the Battenkill, bringing flooding and siltation to drainages whose water had for thousands of years been gently filtered through dense vegetation.

But in these days of the great national guilt trip over how we've messed up the environment, the Battenkill can offer us at least a little comfort. The valley is changing faster than many of us might like, and it does seem to me that the towns are looking more and more like what people from New Jersey and Boston *think* Vermont should look like rather than what Vermont might normally look like. In fact, one former resident complained that all the newcomers, transplanted from the urban complex known locally as BosNyWash, are obsessed with trying to "outquaint each other." But things have improved quite a lot for the river.

After doing a fair amount of historical reading, it became clear to me that nature was having its own way in the Battenkill Valley to a greater extent than at any time since the 1890s. In his excellent book *The Battenkill,* John Merwin, founder of *Rod & Reel* magazine and my successor as director of the museum, offered a stronger assessment. John, whose researches have been much deeper than mine, says it's been getting better since 1800. The clearcutting, the erosion, the various kinds of mills discharging all manner of slop into the river, the routine misuse of the river by an unthinking citizenry, all created a wretched situation that took more than a century to heal.

But heal it did, and even by the late 1800s the river was beginning to receive the acclaim of fishing writers, to the great pleasure of local entrepreneurs, especially the Orvis family. Both Charles, who founded his tackle company in 1856, and his brother Franklin were in the hotel business, and the late Victorian era was the glory days for Battenkill tourism. "Summer people" arrived by train, settled in to the Equinox Hotel and other local establishments, stocked up on tackle at Charlie's shop, and hit the river for some trout fishing.

The forests came back, the streams cleared, and even in the hard times of the Depression, fishermen could at least count on the consolation of good fishing in the "Kill." There were certainly still problems: too much fertilizer and other junk dumped in the river, too much unregulated manipulation of the riverbed, and so on, but the Battenkill had the resilience to handle it.

With the 1960s and the rise of the environmental movement, control and care were more formalized, and threats that had previously been unknown were identified and watch-dogged, often by fishermen: Someone was running his tractor through the river every day, taking a lazy shortcut to a neigh-boring field; someone was digging gravel from the riverbed; someone else was foolishly building a new house in the flood-plain, setting himself up for a wet basement and setting man-agers up for requests to build levees to protect private property. But this river was the product of a pretty harsh natural envi-ronment; it was nothing if not tough, and it continued to at-tract anglers, sightseers, entrepreneurs, and new settlers as its valley attracted ever more intense development and growth. Among these people were more and more friends of the river.

Those friends are going to have to work hard to get along with each other too. More people using the area means in-evitable conflicts. Fishermen and river-floaters (in canoes, in-ner tubes, and other flotation devices) have conflicted in many parts of the country, and though the problem is not yet severe on the Battenkill, it isn't too early to start working on it. A lot of the problem can be solved by a few lessons in manners, but someone has to be giving the lessons, and it has to happen be-fore the conflicts arise.

But it always comes back to this; the Battenkill is a magical place for fishermen, a place that for more than 150 years has been treasured by the best of them as it tested their skills. At the center of this sporting tradition has been the Orvis com-pany, one of the oldest family-owned businesses in the United States. Charles Orvis became the fisherman's equivalent of a household name after the Civil War, for his production of fine rods, an outstanding early reel, and flies that became the closest thing to national standards for quality of production and fidelity to each fly pattern's traditional construction. His daughter, Mary Orvis Marbury, produced one of American fishing literature's milestone volumes, *Favorite Flies and Their Histories* (1892), which not only served generations as the bible of fly patterns but further strengthened the company's reputation for expertise and reliability.

Mary is one of the neglected figures of American fishing history. Though she is known among fishing historians as an important influence on the fishermen of her day—through her book and her management of the Orvis fly department—her actual personality and nature are less clear. She suffered an unhappy marriage, her only son died young, and, after all these years, local stories persist of her as a woman who grew old, bitter, and troubled with alcoholism. She appears to have paid a dear price for success and prominence in what was essentially a man's world.

The Depression almost did in the company, but in 1939 Dudley ("Duckie" to everyone who knew him) Corkran bought Orvis and brought it back to life, restoring its eminence as an important rod builder and a durable New England firm. It was left to a Cleveland businessman, Leigh Perkins, however, to turn Orvis into an internationally known name that represented not only fine fishing tackle but a way of life. Perkins acquired Orvis from Corkran in 1965, and soon the catalogs featured not only rods and flies, but shotguns, clothing, gifts, and other accoutrements of country life. Not surprisingly, quite a few products are named for landmarks in the Battenkill Valley. Leigh is now retired, and his sons Perk and David are running things, and Orvis continues both its commitment to country-lifestyle marketing and to protecting its home river.

But this has not been a one-name river. It has attracted a steady stream of visiting fishermen, some of whom stayed and ultimately were shaped by the challenges of the river and its finicky trout. In the late 1880s, John Harrington Keene, one of the most innovative (if forgotten) of all American fishing writers, lived for some years in Manchester and tested his fly theories on the Battenkill's difficult trout. Lee Wulff, certainly one of the most important forces in twentieth-century fly-fishing, lived for many years along the river in Shushan, New York, just across the state line. In one of my very few conversations with him, he told me a startling tale about 2-pound brook trout the river occasionally yielded to his flies in those years.

John Atherton, a successful commercial artist who, like Norman Rockwell, produced many covers for *The Saturday Evening Post* and other periodicals, lived near Arlington, and the delicately constructed (and even more delicately colored) flies in his beautiful book *The Fly and the Fish* (1951) show the clear influence of the Battenkill and its discriminating trout. When he died, much too young, in 1952, his widow, Maxine, and some friends buried his ashes under a maple along the river.

More recently, a number of important anglers and angler-writers have accepted the challenge of living and fishing on the river. I don't doubt that years from now, young anglers will be speaking in nostalgic tones about the exploits of today's best local fishermen. Come to think of it, I already do. It really is true that the Battenkill is a hard place to catch fish, even though the fish are plentiful. I think it was the late Tony Skilton, for many years director of the Orvis fishing schools, who first pointed out to me that if you can catch fish on the Battenkill, and catch them regularly, you can catch them anywhere. It is what Leigh Perkins calls "Ph.D. fishing."

This is worth explaining, I think, because to the uninitiated it must seem improbable that trout could be much different from stream to stream. For fly fishermen, especially, the Battenkill exemplifies the most complicated meaning of a "good trout stream," that being one that makes you earn its fish. John Merwin recently gave me three reasons why he considers it "one of the most technically difficult brown-trout rivers in the country," confirming my own experience and theories.

First, the water surface is often very flat, and it's perfectly clear, both factors giving the fish all the better a look at your fly. In this way, the Battenkill is similar to the Pennsylvania limestoners: slow moving and glassy, tough to approach and easy to disturb. But it seemed to me that on the Battenkill, even the slickest water was cursed with an amazing number of almost invisible little eddies that threatened to drag a fly and its leader tippet around in ways that alert the fish to fraud.

Second, the fish here have been surviving heavy fishing for 150 years, and the brown trout, introduced late in the 1800s, had been fished hard in Europe for several centuries before that. Conventional wisdom has it that this is why browns are so much harder to catch than native North American wild trout. For centuries the dumber fish were removed from each generation, so anglers were unintentionally managing the fisheries to keep only the least catchable fish in the river, fish that would tend to produce offspring just as smart. To that I add that even the native brook trout, of which the river has many, can be as spooky and uncooperative as the browns. I can't overstate the caution of these fish. One day in early August, Bill Cass, then with Orvis and a talented and careful caster, put a #16 Royal Coachman dry fly over some trout in a still stretch of the upper river; they spooked and fled while the fly was still in the air.

Third, the river's insect populations aren't as dense as in many other streams, so the trout don't rise as freely, giving the fisherman fewer opportunities to cast to them. I fished the up-per river mostly, above Arlington, and it seemed to me that the river downstream of Arlington and on into New York had heavier hatches. I did see a few of what I would call "good" hatches of larger mayflies—and one incredible caddis fly emer-gence just at dark—but the only heavy hatch on the river was the "tricos," the little white-winged black mayflies that appear pretty much clear across the country. Most of the time, mayfly emergences were so light that one May I found it worth writing in my log that I "saw a squadron of about 10 flies go flying up-stream right above the water." Spoiled by the profuse hatches on Midwestern and Western streams, I became pretty sarcastic about the Battenkill's sparse bug life, but John is probably right that this ecological reality is one of the reasons the river is so distinguished for its challenging fishing.

I must add a fourth reason, based on my experiences fishing the wide-open spaces of the West. The stream banks, and the streambed itself, are festooned with the most ungodly array of obstacles—trees, weeds, fiddlehead ferns, brush, sunken logs, fencerows, cows—that I've ever seen anywhere, and even making a decent cast is a challenge.

But even those four reasons, as important as they are, have never really satisfied me as sufficient explanation for how tough this river really is. Almost from the first day I fished the Battenkill, I sensed something else going on. I take a fairly em-pirical approach to most things, but I have to admit that the Battenkill defies empiricism. Again and again, fish rose where I didn't expect them to be; fish behaved just a little differently than my experience on many other waters led me to expect. The Battenkill held something back from me, some fundamen-

tal verity—some little and yet profoundly important idiosyn-
crasy that stood between me and the kind of success I expected. Some of my friends will disagree with this, and I must
admit they have the river figured out far better than I do. They
would suggest, politely but firmly, that I just didn't get good
enough to catch the fish. Some might even suggest, sympathet-
ically, that because my heart was still in the West, I never devoted myself seriously to the river and made the kind of
commitment it takes. Could be, but I still think there was more
going on.

My only time of reliable fishing for larger fish was early in
the year, when the river was high and often muddy. Then,
when the fish were a little hungrier and certainly a whole lot
less wary, I dredged a few favorite runs with big streamers and
caught some decent fish—none of the 5- and 6-pound mon-
sters the local bait fishermen were catching at the same time,
but respectable 15- to 17-inchers. At other times, despite the
best efforts of my friends, I wasn't really up to the Battenkill's
expectations.

And my friends sure tried. Craig Woods, then an editor at
Fly Fisherman, just down the road in Dorset, took me fishing
that first summer. On the way to the river in his SAAB ("So
this is Eastern fishing," I marveled to myself), he handed me a
little box with a delicate, hackle-tip rusty spinner he'd tied, explaining that it was the prevailing fly right now. At the river, I
watched him stalk several diffident risers in water that hardly
seemed to move at all, and after a couple of hours, when I unexpectedly hooked a fish, he called to me, "Did you get him on
the spinner?"

"Uh, no, actually I got him on a big black bucktail, about a
size four, I think." A legend, of sorts, was born, and my aesthetic sensibilities were suspect ever after. My exploits with big

weighted streamers and bead-chain-eyed leech patterns 3 inches long reached the ears of my friends, who reserved such flies for striped bass fishing at Martha's Vineyard. The Battenkill's trout deserved better. "Hey, John, I got a fourteen-incher on the Battenkill last night!"

"Oh?" The pained smile of tolerance flashes, followed by a wincing look, like a man bracing himself for a very loud noise, "What did you catch it on?"

"Well, the only thing hatching was this dinky little gnat-looking thing, so I tried a yellow Marabou Muddler, about a size two, I think it was, or maybe a four. I could check if you want . . ."

"Oh no, don't bother on my account. Say, how about those Red Sox, huh?"

They stuck with me, though. One hot July day, Bill Cass and John Harder took me to a stretch of water just above Oscar Johnson's meadow, where the water was so low and still that it looked like amber Jell-O. Bill, a man of extraordinary generosity, loaned me one of his bamboo rods for the day, a dainty 7-footer for a very light line. It had a Hardy reel that seemed to be about the size of the little zingers I attached to my vest to hold scissors and other necessities. "Hey, lookit this," I effused, while Bill and John grimaced pained smiles of tolerance, "Lookit this teeny little rod! Shouldn't there be a butt section on this end? And lookit this little reel! Look—the spool actually goes around!"

Gradually, I accumulated an embarrassment of tackle like that: microreels and stringy little rods that after a while did seem to cast pretty nicely, even if they did kind of buckle if I tried to double-haul a weighted Woolly Bugger. I learned to tie flies smaller than golf balls, and I even got one of those beautiful Wheatley fly boxes, the ones with all the little transparent

doors so that you can see which flies are in the little compart-
ments where you can't reach with more than one finger at a
time. I learned that a "small fly," rather than being one you
couldn't thread directly onto the fly line, was one that you
couldn't hold far away enough from your face to thread at all.
And though it was not obvious to me at the time, I learned to
fish a whole lot better than I had before.

This didn't dawn on me until I returned to Montana to live
in 1982. Datus Proper invited me over to fish his stretch of
spring creek in the Gallatin Valley, and the day turned into the
sort of story I'd always read in outdoor magazines—the kind
where competent fishermen go out and actually catch fish like
it's a predictable thing to do. We walked down to the lower end
of Datus's property, talking about hatches and tippets and all
those expert things, and as we came to the water, he said, "Let's
see, it's just a little after nine; there ought to be some fish starting to work about now . . . ah, yes, there's one against the near
bank. Here, try this little beetle."

I waded in with my now-worn teeny rod and reel, sized up
the rises, and after a few range-finding casts, I hooked the fish.
"Oh, good work," Datus observed, just as if all this was supposed to happen. I brought the fish in, and Datus checked its
stomach with a marrow scoop, just like famous writers did in
the books. By the end of the day, I'd taken several nice trout,
and I began to wonder if maybe I hadn't learned something on
the Battenkill after all.

I still often think of the Battenkill: of fishing those luxurious
days of high runoff in the new green of spring, when the fish
were eager and strong; of fishing low summer flows in the wilt-
ing heat and humidity, when a lethargic fish might only rise
once every few minutes, and fifteen minutes' careful approach
could be blown by one careless movement; of fishing the late

fall, when all my friends had already switched to grouse hunting, and the river was so full of fallen leaves that every second
or third cast snagged a bright yellow leaf that felt for an instant
like a gentle strike.

Unlike the West, where my favorite fishing came in the last
month of the season, fall fishing was pretty slow for me on the
Battenkill. But New England autumns were every bit the glo-
ries I'd heard they would be. Even with the influx of busloads
of "leaf peepers," it was great fun to drive around through all
that gaudy color. Late one cloudy fall morning, driving up the
Union Street hill from the river to my office, I passed through
a forested slope just as the wind hit it. At the same moment,
the sun emerged momentarily from the clouds, and I was lost
in a thick swirl of flashing golds and ambers, my own Techni-
color ticker tape that glows in my memory long after the day's
fishing has been forgotten.

But then the season would be over, and my disappointment
all the stronger for realizing that the river had pretty much de-
feated me once again. I remember a raw fall morning when I
was still reluctant to let go of fishing for the year and was wondering about driving down to the New York water once more
for another try. Deer season was open, and as I looked out my
cottage window, I saw a pickup truck parked just down the hill
in front of the local store, with two or three unshaven local
men in heavy plaids standing around it. There was a deer
stretched out in the truck's bed, its head hanging over the tailgate, and the men seemed to be just waiting, kind of keeping
company with the deer. They weren't talking, just shivering
and shifting from foot to foot, hunched into their collars. One
of them reached a finger out to the deer and flicked some dirt
from a dun-colored ear.

It was a telling moment, because it suddenly dawned on me

how strong the pull of the Battenkill had become. There was very little excuse to be thinking of fishing. Out there stood some of my neighbors, all of whom had long ago quit fishing for the year, and for at least one of whom even the hunting season was over, and here I was, still trying to talk myself out of another Battenkill summer.

Six

Dry-Fly Culture

A FEW years ago I was driving along the Yellowstone River a few miles north of Gardiner, looking for a good place to fish. As usual, it all looked good, so I chose a spot that also had a nice view. I parked my car, and finding a faint trail, climbed down the high, steep bank to the river. On my way down I noticed another fisherman, a spin fisherman who had spread his gear out on some big rocks and was standing watching the water. There being miles of unoccupied river, I didn't especially mind seeing him and just assumed I'd pass him and walk upstream a ways to some likely spots I knew.

But as I approached him, I noticed that among his other gear was a huge stainless-steel handgun—I thought it might be a Ruger Redhawk .44 Magnum, but it was without question heavy artillery. Even in my abruptly increased caution, I experienced the brief surge of disappointment associated with that class of Guy Moments in which you realize that someone else has brought a toy with him very similar to one that you left at home.

Now, this is Montana. If you run into someone equipped like that, you don't automatically ask him what he's doing; he's likely to be waiting for the commies (or, even worse, the feds) to come up the river in their black gunboats, and he may just wonder if you're some sort of advance recon specialist looking for a skirmish. But as it happened, we struck up a conversation about the fishing, and he seemed pretty normal for a fisherman, so I asked him what he was using the pistol for. He explained that he was "shocking suckers." By spotting a sucker and then shooting right next to it, he could stun the fish. He didn't keep them (a sort of blast-and-release approach). He just stunned them and let them drift away.

The usual response of a high-strung fly fisherman to this sort of behavior might be condescension: What a dumb thing to do! Only a stupid redneck would waste time on something so pointless, instead of the eminently reasonable practice of snagging fish in the mouth with hooks hidden in chicken feathers, playing them to exhaustion, and *then* letting them drift away.

But my own boyhood experiences out on the fringes of sporting propriety asserted themselves. In an instant, I was reminded of my pregunpowder years, when I haunted the brushy margins of a small Ohio town with a BB gun, harassing small birds I would only later come to adore as so much more than targets. The finest moments of that time—that is, the closest I came to approaching something like sport—were spent with a friend, trying to shoot minnows in the local canal. This provided a special challenge, because in order to hit a small, moving minnow, one had not only to lead properly but also to correct for parallax; the deeper the minnow, the bigger the correction. I got pretty good at it.

And so my response to this fellow was sympathetic, if still cautious. "That, uh, sounds like fun." Then, after a brief pause, "Is it legal?"

He took the question well, though it apparently hadn't occurred to him to wonder about such a thing here in Montana. In fact, his reaction was pretty impressive. Rather than pause to worry that he might be breaking the law, he immediately tried to imagine why it *shouldn't* be legal, and the only thing he could come up with by way of objection was that the slugs, lying in fairly shallow water, might find their way into the digestive tract of some other animal, causing lead poisoning. Where we stood, surrounded by high banks, there was no risk of a bullet skipping across the water out into an inhabited area; the banks were too steep. We talked about it a little more, and I moved on. Of course I wondered if he really used the gun for trout too, but I had the good taste not to ask.

I always meant to check to see if there was a Montana law about all this, partly because I remembered that Vermont had a shooting-and-spearing season, during which certain waters were open to shotgunners. They set up tree blinds above the water and took a variety of species—pike, gar, carp, and others, including suckers. But I never did check; I'm not planning to try it, so I don't really need to know, and after all, the joy of this experience was in all the less tangible things it has given me to think about.

As a nature writer, I've devoted a good bit of energy to asserting that we should respect these so-called trash fish as much as any other animals and to wondering why we don't. But here was a wonderfully stimulating approach to the non–sport fish, one I've thought of often since that day I met the sucker shocker. Suckers were appropriate targets because they were good for nothing else. They were biological junk, so they were essentially exempt from ethical consideration; they had no moral context and not enough value for anyone to go after them. We just didn't care, so the fish swam those murky waters out beyond the boundaries of our sporting consciousness.

Then this guy came along and ventured out there onto the frontier of sporting definition and, whether illegally or merely extralegally, pioneered a way to turn suckers into a sporting quarry—a way that even seemed to involve letting them live after he had had his sporting way with them. Very few shooting sports achieve that with live targets.

Over the past several centuries, we have engaged in such adventurism countless times. Every day, someone somewhere is testing a tradition, rearranging a personal sporting code, or simply trying something that seems new but probably isn't. Some of these people are eventually hailed as great pioneers; others just get arrested.

Most such activities go nowhere, of course, because what this or that individual decides to do usually goes no further than his or her local fishing or shooting. Each of us has very little effect on the greater flow of sporting consciousness. But if there is any general pattern to the way sport has gone through this process of evolution, it is toward greater and greater specialization. Witness the "general" fishing rod popular in the mid-1800s, described in chapter three; no one would dream of having only one rod for all the kinds of fishing we regard as technically distinct today. Or, at the opposite extreme from the slugs used by the sucker shocker, consider the dry fly.

First, consider received wisdom about the dry fly as it came down to me when I started fly fishing twenty-five years ago.

According to fly-fishing's leading authorities at that time, such as John Waller Hills in his charming *A History of Fly Fishing for Trout* (1921), and Arnold Gingrich in his more recent but even more cordial *The Fishing in Print* (1974), the dry fly had what amounted to a creation event. According to these genuinely distinguished fishing writers, that moment came in an earlier fishing book (no surprise here), G. P. R. Pulman's *Vade Mecum of Fly Fishing for Trout*, the 1851 edition, published in London. In this book, the author provided what many later fishing writers declared to be the first full description of the dry fly:

> Let a dry fly be substituted for the wet one, the line switched a few times through the air to throw off its superabundant moisture, a judicious cast made just above the rising fish, and the fly allowed to float towards and over them, and the chances are ten to one that it will be seized as readily as the living insect.

What Hills and Gingrich were recognizing in this description were the basic elements of a highly formalized code of how a dry fly should be fished, a code further developed and popularized later in the nineteenth century by one of fly-fishing's most eminent authors, Frederick Halford, whose first book, *Floating Flies and How to Dress Them*, was published in 1886 and took the upper-crust world of British fly-fishing by storm. According to the approach adopted and championed by Halford in a series of progressively more intolerant books, dry-fly fishing was fairly restrictive: You cast only upstream to a specific fish seen to be rising to a natural fly on the surface, and you did so with artificial flies tied specifically to float and be easily dried by false casting—flies with upright, split wings (that is, a pair of wings perpendicular to the hook shank, but leaning somewhat apart from each other), to imitate the upright wings of adult mayflies.

At its height early in the 1900s, this particular view of the origin of dry flies was nearly an absolute thing among dry-fly enthusiasts. As Conrad Voss Bark wrote in *A History of Fly Fishing* (1992), these people "believed, in their sudden blinding conversion and enthusiasm for the dry fly, that this had happened exclusively and entirely on the chalkstreams of Hampshire and that throughout the rest of the country everyone naturally fished the wet fly, the sunk fly, and mostly downstream."

What actually happened was a lot more involved and, therefore, more interesting. It isn't that Halford and his cronies didn't develop a highly refined approach to fishing flies on the surface, and it isn't that people didn't flock to follow their definition of a dry fly. It's that this level of specialization grew out of something very old and much more open-minded.

Fishing writers who take on history tend to be very deterministic. Most of earlier fly-fishing theory and practice is seen as upward progress toward today. Thus, to Halford's many admirers, all that preceded him was just a slow fumbling toward the ultimate glory of Halfordian theory. And thus anything written earlier must be seen through the perceptual filter of people who believed themselves to rest in honor, fulfilled and perfected, at the end of the evolutionary line. This is how they read Pulman, though even a casual reading of Pulman's advice indicates that he wasn't actually struggling toward any particular enlightenment. As Bark, I, and others have pointed out, Pulman has been misread, or wishfully read, to say things he didn't say.

For example, though Hills and later writers gave Pulman credit for first describing false-casting the line to dry the fly, Pulman said no such thing. He started by telling us to put on a fresh fly that is dry. Being dry, why would it need to be false-cast in the first place? Then he told us to false-cast the line, which, being made of woven horsehair or some combination of hair and silk, would eventually get heavy with water; it is the *line's* "superabundant moisture" we are attempting to throw off, not the fly's. Then he told us to cast it over the fish (he never really said we must cast upstream), but referred to the fish as "them," so he was not advising us to pick out a single fish, an absolute requisite of Halford's technique and code. Pulman's description sounds more like fishing over an area known to have some fish, in hopes of inducing one of them to rise; it sounds, in short, positively American.

Some of this I pointed out in *American Fly Fishing: A History,* but since that book was published, a number of writers have improved on our understanding of how the dry fly developed. I think of myself as a fairly hard-core fly-fishing enthusiast, but I'm an innocent bystander compared to guys like Bark and Jack Heddon, who are British, and John Betts, who is American. These three writers have immersed themselves in the earlier fishing literature, attempting to duplicate not only the flies but the rest of the tackle of anglers who lived centuries ago. One of their most startling discoveries involved where these venerable ancients would have fished their flies. Contrary to Hills, Gingrich, and others who simply disregarded frequent mentions by pre-Pulman writers of fishing on the surface, our modern antiquarian anglers realized that these earlier fishermen might have had trouble doing much else. Here's Bark:

As an experiment some years ago, I made a Berners-type rod from a roach pole and parts of old cane rods. That was comparatively easy but the difficulty was making a horsehair line. It took several days to find the willing horse and several more to twist or plait a tapered line. Eventually I had a rod about 16-foot long and a line of about the same length tapered from something like twelve or fourteen hairs at the butt to three at the point [the end the fly is tied to]. . . .

I could cast the horsehair line not only across the wind but against it, providing the wind was not too strong, which experts had told me was impossible with hair lines. It wasn't impossible at all. . . .

What I had not realised and what the experts had not told me was that a hair line cannot sink. The fly did not have sufficient weight to pull it down. It remained visible in or just under the surface film. In modern parlance it was behaving like an emerger.

We also know that fifteenth- sixteenth- and seventeenth-century anglers were savvy enough to weight a fly if need be, so there was nothing stopping them from fishing deep. The point is that there was nothing stopping them from fishing on the surface, either. Their writings reveal that they understood that fish rise to the surface and that insects float on the surface, so they in fact cast their flies to float there too. We have no way of knowing what percentage of the time they spent fishing on the surface, but it seems safe to presume that they would do it whenever it seemed the most promising approach, such as when fish were breaking the surface, feeding on floating insects.

Within the technological limitations of their ages, these fishermen made their flies float. Without the stiff hackles and finer hooks prescribed by Halford to promote flotation, they may have had more trouble keeping their flies on top, but we're limited to what a few fishing books tell us about how they fished, so we have no way of knowing how many fishermen in each century may have actually been practicing some more complete version of Halford's code. We tend to underestimate our ancestors at every turn; their eyesight was as good as ours, and they could no doubt see fish rising and find ways to encourage that behavior toward artificial flies.

So what did happen in the nineteenth century that gave us Halford and his rigid dry-fly code? A number of people, including Pulman and Halford but also including other British writers, such as H. S. Hall, Francis Francis, David Foster, and Halford's mentor and silent partner, G. S. Marryat, refined and formalized an array of traditional practices into something much less flexible. In turning the floating fly, which was intuitively employed by many generations of fly fishermen, into the dry fly, which was by their definition a pretty limited device, they set fly-fishing on a course of increasing specialization and internal rivalry it had not experienced before.

Of course not all these men may have had any such limitations in mind. Most of them were known to like a variety of fishing techniques. But most of them were not possessed of Halford's passion for rigorous definition, nor his flair for promotion. It is Halford's peculiar legacy that, at the same time that he raised a certain technique of fly-fishing to rarefied new heights of success, he attached to it a snooty air of superiority that, though not justified in reality, became a part of fly-fishing culture. By the early 1900s, writers on both sides of the Atlantic would tout dry-fly fishing as the finest, highest form of angling, and Halford's crowd would have decided that in the streams they controlled, it was going to be the *only* kind of fly-fishing.

But the insufferable snobbery of the dry-fly purist and his long and sometimes mean-spirited quarrel with wet-fly and nymph enthusiasts is another story. I am much more attracted to this first period, in which the dry fly emerged and became a kind of icon. What Hills and later writers gave us is one of fly-fishing's great creation myths, almost as satisfying for its cloying tidiness as the myth of Juliana Berners and the Treatise. And what I find especially intriguing about the dry-fly creation myth is how it is actually in a way true.

Scholars of religion and ancient literature define the creation myth as "a cosmogony, a narrative that describes the original ordering of the universe." David and Margaret Leeming explain it this way in A *Dictionary of Creation Myths* (1994):

> Like all myths, creation myths are etiological—they use symbolic narrative to explain beginnings because the culture at one point lacked the information to explain things scientifically. In such myths, then, we find origins of certain recognizable rites, of places and objects sacred to the culture. . . . A creation myth conveys a society's sense of its particular identity; it reveals the way the society sees itself in relation to the cosmos.

Now I know this is pretty high-flown talk to apply to something as seemingly pedestrian as fishing, but in the twenty years or more since I first raised eyebrows by referring to fly-fishing as a subculture, it has become more and more apparent to me that this sport, like most other institutionalized activities in which humans engage, mirrors the same human impulses that other, more formally recognized elements of society do. Just as large corporations and government agencies are recognized for having and cultivating their own internal societies, so do many other common-interest groups generate among their enthusiasts, whether Trekkies or Cubs fans, a separate world of ideas and values.

As the twentieth century has ground along, each generation of fishing writers has described our forefathers in more reverent terms. In the history of the dry fly, Halford (and one of his American counterparts, Theodore Gordon) has taken on very nearly messianic proportions; if not a creator, he was at least a savior, according to his admirers, and it must be admitted that in fact he *was* engaged in creation.

Because what Halford did was turn chaos into order. To that point, all those people who were floating flies in one way or another were just doing it intuitively, because it worked or made sense. They weren't developing anything like a system. Halford, with a Victorian, almost imperial, enthusiasm for precision and definition, managed to develop rules. It was a turning point for the sport. Fly-fishing somehow stumbled along for centuries without many rules, or codes of practice, or widely recognized beliefs about what was and was not sporting. But with Halford and the rise of the formally defined dry fly, we see a heightening of discrimination between different styles of fly-fishing. There were glimpses earlier, of course, and there must always have been competing theories about what worked best, just as there long seems to have been a feeling among fly fishermen that they were doing something with a little more panache than what the bait fishermen did.

But it took Halford and his cronies to endow fly-fishing with hierarchical superiority to its full potential. So firmly did the fly fisher's desire for this kind of regimentation take hold that by the 1920s even a Halford detractor like Hills could look back on Pulman's mid-nineteenth-century remark about how to fish a floating fly and eagerly misinterpret it as a founding statement, one of the pivotal moments in the sport's history. Ironically, what Halford also did was take an open-minded sport in which most practitioners were probably versatile and replace it with a far more fashion-conscious sport in which many practitioners inherited a judgmental tradition with lots more opportunities for the gentle bigotries of style.

Like anyone else who reads too much and fishes too little, I find myself in a continuous conversation with these earlier generations of fishermen. When I took up the sport, I immediately began to read all the books I could find, both new ones and the oft-recommended "classics" written by earlier generations of writers. Out of this gush of discordant advice and flagrant overmarketing came a general position on angling, a code of principles that only actual fishing could correct and bring into alignment with what actually happened on the stream.

At the time, for example, beginner's books made it clear that dry flies were fished upstream and that, in fact, it was impossible to do otherwise. As I thrashed around on the stream, doing intuitive things like millions of anglers before me, I eventually could not escape the feeling that, brilliant though their learning and essays sometimes were, some of these expert guys I was reading must not have met any of my local trout. Again and again, usually through incompetence, I was confronted by nonbook realities: dry flies that sank miserably and then were finally taken by eager fish; or a long dry-fly drift that continued well downstream from me and was taken either just at the end of its drift or, even more disconcerting, after it had begun to drag across the current; or flies in the accidental tradition of George Gibson's half-disassembled wet fly—cheap, straggle-bodied things, with detached hackles trailing along behind, mysteriously taken by fish after fish; or an especially awkward back cast that brought the dry fly to rest on the water behind me just long enough to be grabbed by a trout. I recognized the odd feeling of being embarrassed by these trout—I had not caught them the right way and had therefore betrayed the experts. But even more, I then recognized that I could catch fish using these same techniques on purpose, and that intention made it okay.

I'm still sorting this out. One of the integral parts of the dry-fly creation myth was that it took the development of the split cane fly rod, which was perfected in the years after the American Civil War, to make the Halfordian dry fly a practical fishing tool. According to this story, older rods, made of solid wood, were not powerful enough to fight the breezes and deliver the dry fly with enough precision to the fish's feeding lane. To some extent I've already given away the truth here; the horsehair lines and long rods mimicked by Conrad Voss Bark and his fellow reenactors prove that the dry fly can be fished with a lot of rods. But I had to learn this for myself.

About fifteen years ago, late one May in Vermont, the Battenkill was still high but getting clear. Not long before, Orvis had offered its customers a limited edition greenheart rod, a beautiful, heavy, walnut-colored thing that I fell in love with. I splurged and got one. Honoring tradition and the fact that the rod was made from blanks Orvis had acquired in England, I put a Hardy Perfect reel on it, heavy enough to balance the thick wooden rod, and took it to the river. I knew I wouldn't use it much—it seemed a little too important for actual fishing—but I did want to know what fishing solid wood was like.

My favorite stretch was known as School Bend, a spot where

the Orvis Fishing School instructors took their classes to show them some basic techniques. I favored it partly because it was one of the few places with lots of room for low back casts. All I had to do was watch for the friendly horses and a few bushes here and there. This evening the river was quiet. The banks were still a little raw and muddy from the high water, but the river was clear. Various flies went by in singles and pairs, the way they do on the Battenkill—a mayfly, a couple caddis flies, a yellow stone fly of some sort—but I had already decided what to use. I was experimenting with big spiders, just a short hook with a very large hackle and a tail; no body, no wings. Locals said you couldn't catch fish with them on the Battenkill, but I knew from the box of perfectly tied ones in the John Atherton Collection at the museum that at least one past local expert thought you could.

Mine was made with a badger hackle, very light yellow, almost 2 inches in diameter. I was unable to "skate" it on its hackle tips across the surface as the experts recommended, but when it hit the water and gently flopped over on its side, it seemed attractive enough to the fish. There were some large crane flies around, and it could be the fish mistook it for one of them.

This was my first experience casting the greenheart rod, though I knew from casting a variety of other replicas and privately owned antique rods that it would probably work just fine. Greenheart was the wood that seemed to persist among solid-wood rod traditionalists well into the twentieth century, long after the rise of the split cane rod took the fishing market by storm between 1870 and 1900. The rod had a slow, almost ponderous action that I found quite satisfying, and it had more than enough power to move the big fly anywhere I chose. Precision was not a problem, at least no more than it was for me with any other rod.

I put the spider over a couple of risers who rejected it, then hooked and landed an 11-inch brown that jumped twice in midstream. This was all pretty exciting, first fish on a new rod and all, so I stopped long enough to walk across the road to a friend's house and brag. When I returned, I saw a larger fish rising so close to the far bank, maybe 35 feet away, that his rise form washed up on the bank and splashed on dry dirt. My first cast was just short; he took a real insect just inches from my spider as it passed him. The next cast was better, and he took it, ran deep to midstream, and held there. I had no idea what this rod could take, but it had no trouble with the big bend the fish gave it. Skirting some horses that had wandered my way, I followed the fish downstream, climbed down a few feet of bank to a little grassy ledge about the size of my feet, and flopped the fish, a fat 16-incher, onto it. The fly was firmly embedded in the roof of its mouth.

As soon as I had released the fish, I walked again, much faster, to my friend's cottage, where he welcomed my much grander bragging with a beer. It turned out to be the most memorable fish I caught in five Battenkill summers. Not the largest, or the hardest to catch, but the most satisfying— caught on special gear, with an unorthodox fly, and handled about as well as I ever handled a fish. You never know for sure what you'll remember, but I knew right away about this one.

It was some years later before I realized that I had demonstrated another flaw in the dry-fly creation myth. It is possible to make a decent fly rod out of many kinds of wood. Bamboo may make a better rod, but it isn't magic wood that changed the course of history; it only contributed to a trend then underway. Just a few weeks before writing this, I took the greenheart rod to the Firehole here in Yellowstone and had a great day with it. Again, with several fish rising within casting distance,

I was able to place a small dry fly in their feeding lanes, handle them just fine on the light tippet, and in every other way act like an authentic dry-fly fisherman.

The dry fly is just the kind of development that most sports and other human endeavors experience now and then, something new, like the Beatles or Michael Jordan, in which a shift occurs and things are never quite the same. In 1867, when Candy Cummings became the first person known to throw a curveball in a professional baseball game, there was quite an uproar. I can't imagine that others before him hadn't noticed that a ball curved in flight if it was hit hard enough, or thrown just a certain way, but however it arrived, suddenly the curveball was a big deal; many opposed it as unsporting, just as Halford regarded sunk flies as poor sport, and later writers would cry for the banning of spin fishing as unsporting. Perhaps change in sport, as in nature, is often episodical rather than gradual; perhaps we go along on minor refinements for long periods of time, then abruptly confront some grander change only now and then. The curveball and the dry fly would seem to suggest so. They, and the different attitudes and approaches that grew from them, changed those two sports as significantly as if it were suddenly announced that NFL linemen were allowed to use hatchets on fourth down.

When these developments come, whether or not we understand them at the time and whether or not we mythologize them later, we are undeniably affected by them, even if only through our reaction against them. Orthodoxy reaches to something in our nature and impels some of us to iconoclasm. Halford's rigorous definitions therefore had a great deal to do with the efforts of those who opposed him, from Skues's simple little nymph patterns, to the constructions of the host of modern fly theorists who, disappointed with the structure and performance of the standard dry fly, have reattached its materials at every imaginable angle and spot on the hook in order to build a better dry fly, and then, once it was on the water, manipulated it in every imaginable way, contrary to Halford's admonitions that the fly must float straight with the current.

There is no slackening in our struggle with the dry fly, and I'm not sure there ever could be as long as fishermen keep thinking. There is so much to consider in this matter of imitating a floating insect, and so many variations on the actual experience of convincing trout to rise to a dry fly, that we should never run out of things to puzzle over. I remember a heavy mayfly hatch on Michigan's Au Sable some years ago. As sometimes happens when there are lots of insects about, the swallows were occasionally picking flies off the water, swooping in and grabbing one here and there. Many fishermen have had the experience of a swallow grabbing their artificial, a nice compliment from nature even if not as nice as a trout taking it, and it happened that day. A swallow picked up my brother's fly and carried it a few feet before something, perhaps the drag of the tippet, told the bird that this was not a regular bug, and it dropped it. But as the fly fluttered back to the water, a brown trout came up and took it, almost catching it in the air before it hit the water. At the time we joked that it would be great if we could teach a swallow to do that on command, over good trout.

A less satisfying if no less thought-provoking episode occurred more recently on the Gallatin River south of Bozeman. The salmon fly hatch was on, and these big flies, among nature's most meaty and tempting trout foods, were fluttering high over the river and shore in good numbers. As I watched, one came down with an attractive splash in a quiet stretch of water only a few feet in front of me. It banged its wings on the surface and churned up little ripples in a most attractive commotion, usually irresistible to trout.

Sure enough, after a minute or so a rainbow rose from the rocky bottom and put his nose under the fly to take a good look at it. Then, after a few seconds of scrutiny, the fish threw all dry-fly theory out the window and rejected the real thing, returning to his rocky shelter. We who yearn toward better dry flies should take considerable comfort in this; if on occasion even Nature can't get the pattern and the presentation quite right, who can expect much from us?

Seven

ROYAL COACHMAN
AND FRIENDS

B O U T two weeks before writing this, I was in Bud Lilly's car on the way to a Montana spring creek he had recently discovered, an unknown treasure of a place to which he was one of very few people with access. As I've already said, these little creeks, whether in the limestone country of Pennsylvania, the lava lands of Idaho, or here in the broad basins of western Montana, are special to fly fishermen because they hold big, smart trout. From what Bud told me, this little stream was outstanding even among this class of water; two weeks earlier, he watched a friend take a 26-inch brown trout on a dry fly.

I'd read about places like this; we all have. And though I've fished a lot of really special streams, including some great spring creeks, I've never been on one where there was much chance of interesting such a huge fish in such a small fly. In my experience, such fish were too smart, their appetites were too large, and their numbers were too small for there to be any statistical likelihood of encountering one, even on the best-managed spring creeks. Fish that big were caught on dry flies only in the pages of books by people who fished creeks nobody else fished. I knew there were places like that too, but I didn't ever expect to be going to one.

With all this racing through my mind, I tried to imagine what sort of exacting presentation and tricky little fly pattern it must have taken to hook a 26-incher. "What did he take it on?"

As he drove me toward this magical place, Bud took off his hat, said, "He took it on this," and spun the hat so that I could see, firmly hooked to the band, a #10 Royal Wulff.

"Oh." Once again, tradition and prettiness had triumphed over technology and entomology. The ghost of the Royal Coachman was alive and well in the Gallatin Valley.

My biggest fish that day was "only" 22 inches long. I caught it on a grasshopper imitation, and in a stream 6 feet wide it looked like a salmon and exercised my considerable expletive vocabulary for quite some time before I landed it. As I released it and prepared to cast again, for only the second time in all my fishing I was mildly afraid of what might happen when I did. That and several other fish (Bud called my first fish, a 15-incher, "one of the little ones") amounted to the most exhilarating morning of dry-fly fishing I'd ever experienced.

But on the way home, I thought about one enormous bow wave that rushed up to my fly and then collapsed as the fish turned away; it happened right about where Bud said the 26-incher lived. If only I'd had a Royal Wulff.

⬧

An extraordinary change overtook fly tying after the Civil War, even before the dry fly came along. While American anglers in the early 1800s seemed to choose their flies from a relatively modest number of known patterns (mostly British) and a few local variants, the great boom in the recreational industry following the Civil War generated countless new patterns. As sporting periodicals were launched, dozens of fishing and hunting clubs were organized, and as the commerce of everything to do with outdoor recreation accelerated, so did the pace of change and the demand for something new. American anglers, blessed with tremendous diversity of fishing waters and a wealth of easily accessible fly-tying materials, became folk artists, creating new fly patterns and variations on old fly patterns and then championing them among their friends and the larger community of fishermen who kept in touch in the pages of *Forest and Stream, American Angler, American Field,* and many other periodicals.

But it was a different sort of enterprise than we see in today's fly market. No doubt some of these fly boosters hoped, as do many modern innovators, to make money, and no doubt, like today's tiers, they may also have wanted to make a name for themselves. Contributing an enduring fly pattern to the sport may seem an odd bid for immortality, but such is the nature of the fly-fishing passion. What was different back then was that it all mattered a lot less to the fish than it does now.

For the most part, this explosion in new fly patterns did not include an expansion in fly styles. With only a few striking exceptions, most of these new flies were tied in precisely the same style as traditional down-winged wet flies. Though the local creator of a pattern may have intended it to have different proportions—a longer wing, say, or some unusual body shape—if the pattern was among the rare few that were noticed by the professionals and made it into commercial production, odds were good it would be standardized to the proportions and shape of all the other mass-produced flies of the time. But, however disappointing this might have been to the originator of the fly, it worked that way because the standard proportions and shape would work just fine. When the fish were hitting, as they often were, especially in the more lightly fished waters, the fly would still work.

For all the efforts of our most inspired fly-tying empiricists, it is simply impossible to remove all the mysticism from flies. Fish are responding to so many stimuli we aren't aware of, using senses we don't fully understand, that even with the most naive wilderness trout, every cast is kind of a crapshoot. Between 1860 and 1890, that is, before the European brown trout became widespread and forced anglers to attend to natural fish foods in choosing their fly patterns, arguments over which was the best fly were less focused on things like how well each fly imitated a living creature and more on what might almost be called aesthetic issues. Was a dark fly or a bright fly better? Was a blue wing better than a red one; was some combination of colors the answer? Why did bass like purple so much, and what was this new theory I just heard about yellow?

I don't mean to suggest that these fishermen were stupid, or unaware; some of them, purely through personal observation, were already laying the groundwork for most of the fly types we use today, including imitations of bait fish, frogs, nymphs, and floating flies. I would suggest, however, that most of them, because of the kinds of fishing they did, for brook trout, bass, and other fairly undiscriminating fish, were playing by other rules. They could afford to debate the relative merits of a green versus a red tail on their favorite lake fly.

No fly better represents this freewheeling era in fly tying

than the Royal Coachman, which, among the general public, may be the world's best-known fly. Its name has the right combination of romance and class to appeal even to people who don't fish, and the fly has such a commanding appearance that few fly fishermen can resist having some permutation of the pattern in their fly boxes, even if they never use it. Most of them don't know it, but the Royal Coachman is the first great American fly pattern and is both emblematic of the flowering of a distinctly American type of fly tying and symptomatic of what eventually caused that movement to collapse.

It's only partly American, of course. It's a variation of an older British pattern, the less flashy coachman, which was originated by Tom Bosworth, coachman to George IV, William IV, and Victoria. Among the peculiar lore sustained in fishing literature is Bosworth's precision use of the coachman's whip, with which, according to David Foster in his *Scientific Angler* (1885), Bosworth could "take the pipe from the teeth of a passing pedestrian," an accuracy reportedly transferred to his skilled use of a fly rod:

> As a successful fisherman, old Tom, when known to the writer, was unsurpassed. He would often fish in the wake of several rodsters, whose energy would succeed their skill, and would extract, not infrequently, three times over the weight of fish, by skillful and careful casting over the awkward and most unlikely-looking spots, which the majority of anglers would never dream of trying.

Bosworth apparently developed his coachman, a simple fly with a white wing and a peacock-herl body, for night fishing; the contrast between the bright wing and the dark body was supposed to make the fly more visible. It was mentioned in

Salter's *The Angler's Guide*, as early as the 1825 edition, and became a mainstay of British fishing manuals throughout that century, recommended in a variety of sizes and materials.

A complaint among late-nineteenth-century fly enthusiasts was the impossibility of keeping up with new patterns, or even knowing when a slight variation in an existing pattern justified a new name. The Royal Coachman epitomizes that problem too, for it had only one feature—its scarlet band—that distinguished it from Bosworth's pattern. As Datus Proper pointed out in *What the Trout Said* (1982), the only real difference between the Royal Coachman and the ant pattern in W. H. Aldam's *A Quaint Treatise on Flees, and the Art of Artyfichall Flee Making* (1876) was the color of the wing. Who can measure the variables that make one fly so famous while thousands of others are forgotten?

It was first tied in about 1878 by John Haily (sometimes spelled Hailey), a professional tier in New York. Haily was at that time a tier for Charles Orvis, who later wrote about the origin of the Royal Coachman in *Forest and Stream*, February 5, 1885:

> In looking through my fly-case I often call to mind the history of each variety, and I sometimes wonder if a little memorandum of the same would in time become of interest.
>
> The royal coachman . . . was first offered to purchasers by me. It did not, however, originate with me. The fly-tyer I mentioned long ago sent me a sample of the same, saying, "I have just been tieing some flies to order for a gentleman. He says he likes the coachman better than any other fly, but he finds it very frail, and he wants me to tie some with red silk in the middle, to make them stronger, and he also wants a little sprig of wood duck for a jib (tail). I send you a fly to see. I think it quite handsome."

This inclosed fly had a white wing, brown hackle, peacock body, bound in the center with red silk, and tail of wood duck feather with the black and white bars. I kept this fly for some time, showing it to several people. One evening a number were gathered around a table looking at the flies. My family, Mr. Horace T. Dunn, of California, and Mr. L. C. Orvis, of Hartford, Conn., were present discussing the propriety of every fly having a name, numbers giving them little or no individuality. I said, "But what is one to do? I do not propose to name flies. We have too many already." "Why not?" say they. "If you make a new combination name it. Else it will never be popular. No one can remember to distinguish flies by numbers; they get confused. A name fixes a fly in your mind." "Well," I answered, "that may be; but look, here is this fly, a handsome fly; it is similar to a coachman, but it is not a coachman. There is but one coachman; that is the fly we all know, with a white wing, peacock body and brown hackle."

"I will tell you," exclaimed Mr. L. C. Orvis, "that is an extra fine coachman; all that scarlet makes it quite magnificent— call it—call it—the royal coachman." This seemed suitable, so the fly was christened. Not long after I published a list of flies, and included the "royal" coachman in the number.

Later I received a letter from an angler in Wagon Wheel Gap, Colorado, saying: "I wish you would make a coachman for me with all the gilt on it possible. I believe such a fly would be stronger and more taking."

We tied the flies, making the body of gilt, with only a neck or ruff of peacock herl, and it proved most acceptable both to the man for whom it was designed and to the fish of Colorado. We have made many dozens for that country, and it seemed too good a fly not to be added to the list, so the "gilt" coachman received a place.

The red-tip coachman and lead-wing coachman had been known in the trade long before I entered it, but I feel responsible for the innovation of the royal and gilt coachman, and here confess and account for the same.

We can see the people at Orvis, one of the leading mail-order fly dealers and eventually the foremost arbiters of turn-of-the-century fly aesthetics, in an interesting struggle here. The flow of new patterns was annoying and chaotic; should we just give them all numbers? If so, who gets to assign such numbers? Charles Orvis knew as well as anyone that fishermen would not be stopped from their incessant tinkering and modifications, but he was uneasy about the point of such an unruly process, even though it was making him money.

Today the Royal Coachman seems a bit of an oddity, a survivor from a gaudier and more innocent time. The band of silk floss in the middle of the body sets it apart from almost all modern patterns. But in the 1890s, many trout and bass flies were tied like it. In Mary Orvis Marbury's milestone book *Favorite Flies and Their Histories*, published in 1892, there were nearly thirty fly patterns that featured colorful bands of material with tufts of herl or chenille at the butt in the manner of the Royal Coachman. Most of them are long forgotten, further evidence that there is something special and durable about the fly that Haily invented.

Almost as soon as American fly fishermen began writing about fly tying they began trying to imitate local stream insects. Early angler-entomologists included Robert Barnwell Roosevelt and Sarah McBride, both of whose writings influenced later fly tiers. None of the later ones is more famous than Theodore Gordon, the well-known Catskill fly tier. Gordon was one of many turn-of-the-century fishermen who experimented with new fly patterns as wary brown trout replaced brookies in hard-fished streams, and so he was one of the first commentators to bring a new perspective to flies like the Royal Coachman. For some years he believed that it imitated an ant, but late in life he decided that was unlikely. In 1914, he wrote to fellow fly tier Roy Steenrod that "what the trout takes R. Coachman for, I cannot imagine. I do not use it, except when the water is colored, but a lot of men do, and kill with it." Gordon became perhaps the first angler to resist using this colorful pattern because it just didn't *look* like anything. Many later anglers, especially those devoted to matching a specific insect hatch, would have the same problem. To the hard-core hatch matcher, the Royal Coachman was, in the words of Ted Leeson, "an act of aesthetic vandalism, a grotesque violence perpetrated on a fly box." The Royal Coachman didn't make sense to these people because they couldn't imagine how it made any sense to trout. That trout took it, often quite greedily, was not reason enough for many fishermen, then or now.

Gordon has been given credit for first converting it to a fanwing dry fly, which may explain his comparing it to an ant; flying ants are often consumed by rising trout. There was at the time a nationally popular fly called The Ant (a slight variation on Aldam's version, mentioned above) that was quite similar in general coloring to the Royal Coachman, though by modern standards neither of them look much like any known insect.

In the 120 years since Haily mailed his sample fly to Orvis, the Royal Coachman has been reworked countless times, almost beyond recognition. The fly has had no rest at the hands of succeeding generations of fly tiers. It became a fat, bulky bass fly; a long, graceful featherwing streamer; an equally long bucktail, an Atlantic salmon fly; a steelhead fly, even a midge. And there are dozens of anonymous versions that have shown up in the boxes of anglers: bivisibles, double-wings, humpies, nymphs, flies with *two* red bands instead of one—every imaginable variation. America's romance with this versatile pattern shows no sign of letting up. Lee Wulff made the most famous and useful modification many years ago, replacing the wings and tail with white hair and creating the Royal Wulff, a tremendously popular rough-water pattern.

(It is probably predictable that even the Royal Wulff has a complicated patrimony. In 1930, the great Catskill fly tier Rube Cross tied a hair-*winged* Royal Coachman for a Beaverkill fisherman friend, L. Q. Quackenbush. It became known as the Quack Coachman, in Quackenbush's honor, and though it had white hair wings, it still had the hackle-fiber tails of the original Royal Coachman. It is unclear to me whether Wulff based his own version [created about the same time] on this pattern or whether the two patterns emerged independently; perhaps some reader knows more.)

But fly-fishing entomology continued to advance, and finally part of the mystery of the fly's success was solved. Preston Jennings, whose *Book of Trout Flies* (1935) at last codified some of the important insect hatches on Eastern trout streams, recognized the fly's gross similarities to the *Isonychia* mayflies. In an article in *Esquire* in 1956 entitled "There IS a Royal Coachman," he explained that a Royal Coachman wet fly worked quickly through the water could well imitate the quick-swimming motion of the energetic *Isonychia* nymphs. Arnold Gingrich, at that time publisher and editor of *Esquire*, later devoted a chapter in his *Well-Tempered Angler* to Jennings's discovery, suggesting that the least we could do for such a breakthrough is elect Jennings President. Jennings modified the pattern in several ways, actually developing his own nymph version of it.

But as anyone who has used the pattern much knows, the *Isonychia* theory doesn't explain it all. In fact it only explains a little. Like most good flies, the Royal Coachman often works well even when there are no insects in the water that look anything like it. In his small masterpiece, the *New Streamside Guide* (1947), Art Flick made a good attempt to explain the Royal Coachman. Admitting that he hadn't "the slightest idea what insect the Fan-Wing Royal is supposed to imitate," he suggested that its popularity rests on other factors: It is attractive and therefore sells well; it's easy to see when fishing; it has gotten an extraordinary amount of publicity, therefore everyone feels they must have a few; and it has proven itself valuable for bringing fish up when no insects are emerging, or in heavy water, where fish can see it as well as anglers can.

That's a good start, I think. Many fishermen have noticed that they catch the most fish on the flies they have the most confidence in; that when you believe in the fly you're more attentive and more successful. The corollary of that rule of confidence is that a fly you have little confidence in will catch you fewer fish than one you believe in, even if the former is a better representation of the prevailing insects.

Fishermen still try to justify the Royal Coachman. They still want to believe it looks like something—a dragonfly, a moth, a crippled hummingbird, a lightning bug; there is a desperation in these efforts to label the fly. And it's unnecessary. Trout take flies for lots of reasons we know and for some we'll never understand. They also take cigarette butts, gum wrappers, and baby ducks. The Royal Coachman may look to us like something that just fell off a Christmas tree, but it has inspired confidence in thousands of anglers, and confidence catches as many trout as the right pattern. Among fly patterns, most of which come and go like all other fads, the Royal Coachman is the rare exception: the fly that has not been forgotten. Its longevity is certainly the result of good publicity, sales appeal, and other things that have little to do with a trout's appetites, but no fly lasts that doesn't work. Charles Orvis may have cataiogued it because it was "quite handsome," but his customers kept buying it because they caught fish with it. Maybe knowing that it has worked so often for so long is good enough, and maybe part of its real glamor and appeal is that we *don't* understand why it works. Fishing can use a little of that kind of mystery; a few uncertainties are good for us. The Royal Coachman, like any other good fly, will always have its days, and those days are surely not less rich for a little mystery.

It might be better, however, to say that the *idea* of the Royal Coachman lives on, rather than to say that the fly itself does. A quick run through the current tackle catalogues, or through the local fly shops, suggests that the original fly and even its long-popular dry-fly version are growing less common. What I find instead are its descendants, especially the Royal Wulff. Gary LaFontaine, one of our most determined and convincing fly inventors, admits that for all the energy he has put into creating new and often quite unorthodox flies, the Royal Trude, another Royal Coachman variation with a single back-slanting wing of white hair, was his most effective pattern throughout the 1980s. The Royal Coachman now survives almost entirely in mutated forms; this is not unusual for great flies, which often evolve at the hands of generations of fly tiers, but the mutations have rarely been so pronounced, or the results so universally regarded as superior to the original.

Eight

ARTS AND CRAFTS

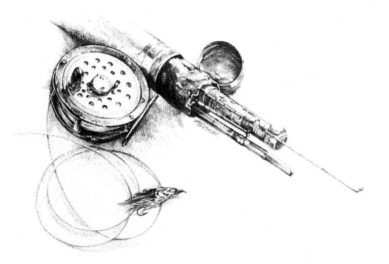

O N E day on one of their all-too-infrequent visits to my office at the museum, Helen Shaw and Hermann Kessler were looking around the collections rooms. Hermann, then retired from *Field & Stream* and occupied with book projects, was offering one of his customarily strong opinions on something or other, and as he spoke, I happened to glance over at Helen.

She had picked up a fly—a Muddler Minnow by an unknown tier—from the worktable where it was being catalogued. Helen had truly earned her title of the "first lady of American fly tying," but she is also a warm, kind person, and we had rarely talked about fly-tying practice (mostly, as I recall, we listened to Hermann). I was unaccustomed to seeing her professional side, and so, just for an instant, I was absorbed in her actions. With the critical eye of an expert, a look I had not seen during our casual conversations, she automatically— almost reflexively—gave the fly a quick once-over. As she held it in one hand, a harder expression passed over her face. She scruffed the deer-hair collar and mentally measured the proportions, or whatever real masters do when they look at someone else's work. As the instant passed and she put the fly back, I thought that there was nothing in the world I would less like to be right then than a poorly tied fly.

An insight like that deepens my respect for the sport in ways I don't claim to fully understand but appreciate immensely. When the great classic rod dealer Martin Keane was trying to acquaint me with the rudiments of antique tackle identification and evaluation, we would have long phone conversations as I tried to figure out this or that new acquisition. One day we were discussing a peculiarly puzzling antique rod. I covered its basic features, describing its fittings and dimensions, and he interpreted my report as credibly as usual.

Then, figuring I was ready for higher things, he said, "Okay, Paul, now forget all that other stuff for a minute and just *look at the rod*. What does it *say* to you? Does it have quality about it? Was there love in its construction, or did someone just throw it together? How does it *feel* to you?" I smiled as I realized that he was doing what some of the best curators in the museum world acknowledge must be done; there must be a level of evaluation beyond mechanical assessment, and it must be carried out with an open mind. It must not be carried out recklessly, or in ignorance, but it is part of the aesthetics of any fine craft.

Ever after, as I opened countless packages containing donations, once in a while I pulled out something—a reel, a rod, even a fly book—that was special, that had the quality we all look for, and even in the haste and fatigue of too long a workday I would think of Marty and how he would appreciate this one.

Only a few weeks before I left the museum, I unwrapped a small parcel containing a single worn fly book of obvious antiquity, assuming it would be like dozens of others, full of half-chewed, undatable, snelled wet flies (and hoping nothing would crawl up my arms as I held it). Instead, it contained the oldest salmon flies I'd ever seen, two of them, on braided silkworm gut, tightly attached to a faded and yellowed tag dated 1835. Another envelope, dated 1824, contained the oldest fly hooks yet acquired by the museum. Both were remarkable finds in a sport where tackle that is much more than a century old is rare.

I wondered at the reasoning of some sport 150 years ago as he carefully inscribed his little leader envelopes and packets with dates, having no way of imagining they would find their way to us. I wonder at all the other fishermen who didn't bother to date their acquisitions. And I wonder why, though I suspect I know, such a find seems so important to modern fly-fishing, even though most modern fly fishers don't know or care about it.

Some of us do care, at least enough to want to think well of ourselves because we are the latest (and presumably brightest) generation in a long tradition. Our writers refer to our fishing ancestors as "storied" and "legendary," and they like to pump us up with flowery talk about the noble heritage of our sport. Fly fishermen are notorious for perceiving themselves as occupying the aesthetic (if not the moral) high ground.

This self-image involves us in some interesting affectations.

For one thing, we tend to regard fly-fishing and its component parts as something better than sport. We think that what we're doing here is art. So far my reading has revealed only Nick Lyons sharing my view, but when it comes to matters literary, I consider Nick a majority of one, and so I'm heartened by the company. He and I seem to agree that the word "art" is terribly overused.

The popular Pennsylvania fishing writer Jim Bashline, in *Atlantic Salmon Fishing* (1987), summed up the pride of achievement fly fishermen feel this way:

> My definition of critics is that they are those people who belong to the "they" group. You know, "they" say that . . . so on and so on. Some of these "they" people say that fly tying is not an art, it's a craft. According to "them" (closely allied to "they"), woodcarving is not an art either. Nor is making paper airplanes or fashioning a functional tool out of hot steel with anvil and hammer. If you've ever been to a duck decoy competition, watched a Japanese origami expert fold paper or a horny-handed blacksmith twist white-hot steel into a swinging gate, you know better. Yes, anyone with reasonable dexterity can tie a fly. The same can be said for painting with oils or fashioning a human likeness from a gob of clay. As in all such endeavors, few practitioners will reach the peak or close to it. The "average" fly tiers are merely that—as are those "average" folks who paint. But an artist is easily recognizable; the great fly tiers are artists. There, that's that.

That's what? Jim's gone now and can't defend himself, but fly-fishing is a multigeneration conversation, so I'll go ahead and speak to him. Jim, this is no argument at all; it misses the entire point of words having definitions in the first place. It's like saying that a cat that gets better and better at being a cat will eventually move up and turn into a dog; or if you raise really great oranges, eventually your orange trees will produce apples. Just because you get better and better at what you do doesn't mean that what you do will become something else. Why should you want it to?

Craft is generally defined as the creation of something whose primary function is utilitarian rather than aesthetic. Craft can involve great creativity and originality, even genius. So can art, engineering, and cooking. A fishing rod is, first, a tool for catching fish. A fly is, first, a tool for catching fish. A cast is, first, a process employed to catch fish. Some of these activities may be practiced so finely as to reach a high level of craftsmanship; some may even be practiced by genuine artisans. But they are crafts. They do not cease to be crafts just because (as in the case of bamboo rods, full-dress salmon flies, or handmade willow baskets) the person who buys them takes them home and uses them as ornaments rather than tools. As the saying goes, just because the cat has her kittens in the oven don't make 'em biscuits.

But, some may object, this artful terminology goes back centuries; look at all the books called *The Art of Angling*. True, but if you look to the libraries of those former days you will discover that the word had a different connotation then. For every *Art of Angling* there was an *Art of Brewing* or *Art of Animal Husbandry* or *Art of Blacksmithing*. Our forebears certainly admired their greatest craftsmen, perhaps as much as they admired their greatest artists, but you can be sure that no one was confusing the local blacksmith with Mozart.

The excellence, even brilliance, of the achievements of a Lee Wulff or a Vincent Marinaro are in no way lessened by giving those achievements their correct name. I imagine I know why this sort of talk goes on, though. It has class. It sets us apart from the people who wouldn't dare call baseball, or bowling, or sailing an art. It is a manifestation of the elitism we like to pretend isn't there (though I wonder; if we as fly fishers think we're so swell and that fly-fishing is really the best sport, why don't we just come out and be elitist about it?).

We also like this kind of talk because, in some arenas, fishermen are involved in art. We benefit from the art of countless photographers, painters, illustrators, sculptors, and writers. Some of us love Schubert's "Trout Quintet," or Gordon Lightfoot's "Rainbow Trout." We are blessed with artists who evoke all that we love about our sport. And we are equally blessed by all the great craftsmen who make our sport so much fun to practice.

One of the most powerful analogies (and at the same time a prodigious conceit) that I've read in fishing writing is the comparing of some rod builder to a violin maker. Such-and-such a rod builder is called the "Stradivarius of bamboo rods," or, even more improbably, the "Guarneri of glass." Now this is nice talk, and no doubt the rod builders in question are at the top of their craft, but it gives a poor impression of the levels of sophistication of violin making and rod building. Comparing a violin built by a master, or even by a mediocre builder, to a fly rod, as if to say that the two products require equal skill to make, is absurd.

We may compare the deep spiritual devotion of the respective craftsmen, perhaps, or their lifelong development of a perfect technique, but that's about all. A violin is an exceptionally complex piece of work, with arches, tensions, and dynamics that do not have equivalents in a fly rod. No matter how much attention and ornamentation we may lavish on it, a fly rod after all is just a stick. Our physical demands on the stick are large, but they are straightforward compared to what we expect from a violin in its numerous delicate parts—fingerboard, neck, sound box, tuning keys, bridge, and so on.

Arnold Gingrich used to make this analogy, despite being a fiddle player himself. He must have known better and must have enjoyed the pleasant compliment he was able to offer to the poor underappreciated, underpaid people who build good rods. Unfortunately, most of his readers took him at his word. Why deny it? We like to think of ourselves as involved in something almost mystically sophisticated, and Arnold just fanned the flames.

Quite naturally the "fine rod snobbery" syndrome has settled most incurably in the hearts of those relatively few people who own bamboo rods. Your average fisherman—the thousands of occasional fly fishermen who wouldn't know Preston Jennings from Waylon Jennings—has probably never used one. That some of the people you see in the outdoor magazines are using them only proves the point; they are the insiders, the people with a seat on the gravy train.

In his outstanding new book *Fishing Bamboo* (1997), John Gierach says that in recent years there has been an increase in bamboo-rod snobbery:

> People who fish bamboo rods are now sometimes seen as a little snooty, where only a decade or two ago we were just thought to be folks who liked good fishing tackle. I can't say the ostentation isn't there at times because, like anything else that can be seen as sort of high tone, bamboo rods do attract their share of people who are wound too tight.

I don't mind telling you that it worries me when I disagree with John, because besides writing such thoughtful and entertaining books, he almost always makes such good sense. I worry about turning into a curmudgeon before my time, becoming cranky and negative about everything, like those poor tormented souls who review movies for *The New Yorker*. But this was the only passage in his entire book I would argue with, so maybe I'm okay for now.

John must hang out with a different crowd from any of those I've known over the past twenty-five years. Bamboo-rod enthusiasts have always had their share of snoots. It goes way back, and I think it headed for new heights as soon as fiberglass rods appeared more than fifty years ago.

I can remember the first "classic" bamboo rod I ever saw, because I've never really recovered from the disappointment. This, I thought to myself, is what everyone is so uppity about? Why, it's almost ugly. Coming to fly-fishing from the lowest end of the market, but with a real love of woodworking (my father, a real craftsman, built most of our furniture and taught me to use all his woodworking tools), I found that my idea of what constituted a "beautiful" rod was all out of line with angling fashion. I'd learned to think of wood as pretty for several qualities: color, grain (direction, intensity, and a characteristic that fellow wood-lovers might recognize if I called it "swing," that flow of the lines as they thicken and bend), luster under polish or finish, how it took a stain, how it aged, and so on.

Bamboo had few of those qualities. It was almost grainless except at nose-length. It was usually a sort of pale straw color, like the cheap pines I had little use for. If it was darker, the darkness was artificial, varnish- or heat-induced; that helped sometimes (Paul Young's rods had wonderful colors), but bamboo lacked just about everything else I admired in a wood. It was boring.

This mattered more to me after I came to the museum. Suddenly I was caretaker of some seven hundred fly rods, representing many of the best names, the most famous owners. I learned a lot more about fly rods and came to admire their builders very much, but my mind did not entirely change. In fact, I discovered that there had been much prettier wood rods a century ago. Lancewood, a soft yellow, sometimes almost brilliant under the right varnish, had a simple brightness I was immediately attracted to. Greenheart, which I've mentioned already, was instantly a favorite; here was a wood with a color I wouldn't have been surprised to see in my dad's wood shop, a rich, deep walnut color. There was ironwood, hazel, hickory, snakewood, and lots of others I couldn't even identify.

But when I saw bamboo rods built by the "greats"—Payne, Gillum, Thomas, Kosmic, Edwards, Orvis, Leonard, and the rest—I had a good enough sense of woodworking craft to recognize them for what they were: superbly produced fishing rods, as fine, delicate, and precise as the human hand and its helpful machines could make them. They're very nice. They're wonderful, in fact. But are they really justification for the caste system they sustain in the minds of those fortunate enough to own them (Gierach and his pals excepted)? Do they deserve adoration, or qualify their owners to ridicule synthetic rods created by what one writer in the 1970s called "the cold chemistry of silicate sand?" Apparently they do, but I don't see why.

These days the good bamboo rods don't do anything better than the "artificial" rods except earn money for whoever sells them. Actually, from what my friends in the business tell me, they don't even do that better. They don't seem to do anything *practical* better. Of course, they don't have to; nobody is claiming that fly-fishing is practical anyway. So why are they better?

You should read John's book to get the whole story, but in essence, bamboo has a "feel" and an action that some fishermen just love. Bamboo appeals to our most subjective, and therefore most important, moods. It doesn't matter at all that some skilled graphite or fiberglass rod builder could, with enough time and money, probably make a rod that duplicates precisely that action; it isn't made of bamboo, therefore it isn't the same. I appreciate this kind of commitment; I feel the same way about cotton versus polyester, or wooden baseball bats versus aluminum ones, or wooden skis versus plastic ones. The great thing about fly-fishing is that we get to make subjective choices and shouldn't feel any need to defend them as long as they don't do anyone any harm.

Now that I think of it, the worst rod I ever used was bamboo. A friend, whom I shall call Bozo because that is what his friends called him, won it at a Trout Unlimited dinner-raffle. Bozo was the terror of the banquet circuit. Every year he picked up a couple of rods or shotguns because of his gift for buying the right raffle tickets. His luck failed him with this rod, though.

It was a Leonard, apparently from an embarrassing period in the company's history when something was going wrong, so that now, if you own one of those rods, people nod and say "Oh, you got one of *those* rods . . ." It was gorgeous, and Bozo would frequently get it out for a few minutes when we went fishing, but he would quickly put it away, muttering to himself in frustration.

But it looked so good, and it was made by one of the all-time great names, so I just couldn't believe it wasn't a good rod. After all, if I could catch fish on a $10 glass rod, how much easier must a $300 (this was almost twenty years ago; it would cost $1,500 now) bamboo rod be? I finally objected. "Boze, you just

don't know how to handle that thing. Look at it—it's great!"
Cosmetics had me convinced.

"Okay, here—*you* try it."

He was right. The rod was impossible. It was supposed to
handle a 6-weight line, and to this day I believe that there was
a section of it, maybe 2 feet long and somewhere near the middle, that was about right for a 6-weight line. Nothing else was,
nor was the rest of it comfortable with any other single line
weight. There was no combination of patience, finesse, timing,
and force that could work more than about 25 feet of line into
the air without risk of torn ligaments. It was like trying to cast
last night's linguini with a screen-door spring.

After a while I found that I could make a fair trout-fishing
cast of maybe 30 feet if I put a weight-forward 3-weight line on
it, but it seemed like a hefty calorie expenditure for the results I
got. By that time my worst preconceptions about bamboo were
reinforced. The sloppiest machines and workmen in the world
could turn out a thousand discount-store glass rods and not one
of them would be as baffling as that rod was. It was an organic
miracle.

Of course most bamboo rods work just fine. I know plenty of
excellent fishermen (certainly better than I am) who swear by
them. They even claim they can detect a difference between
apparently identical rods. Their sensitivities are greater than
mine. They argue over which craftsman's handmade master-
pieces are the best, and they're not just arguing over who has
the prettiest zebrawood reel-seat inserts, or who can do the
fanciest wrapping. (There was a man a few years ago who spe-
cialized in a one-wrap wind, just a single turn of thread around
the shaft, and no matter how hard you looked, you couldn't
find the beginning or the end of that thread; that may be an or-
namental stunt, but it's a truly classy one.) They're arguing

over action, "cushioning," fatigue, and other imponderables.

And I even own a bamboo rod myself now. It happens to be an Orvis, a Seven-Four, and I enjoy it as much as any other rod I have. It's great fun for trout, though I've never taken anything over 18 inches with it, but it's no more fun than an equivalent graphite rod, at least not for me. I'm a nondiscriminating rod user; the rods all cast better than I can, and they're all fun. But then I also like greenheart, which, I suppose, proves I'm just as susceptible to impractical thinking as anyone else.

But I don't think, just because I like some obscure, hard-to-come-by type of rod, that I'm a higher form of human being than my fellow fishermen who use (or weren't lucky enough ever to be able to afford more than) glass rods. That's my problem with bamboo elitism. Nothing wrong with loving the bamboo rod, singing its praises, or writing about it with the heat of a romance author (well, nothing serious anyway). Just don't get the idea that it makes you a better person.

"The thing about a bamboo rod," my brother observed, a few hours after buying his first, "is that it kind of makes you want to buy another one." That's a safe generalization about any fishing tackle, I suppose, but it does seem to have a special truth with bamboo rods. They are bought with guilt, snuck home or hidden in the trunk, and hoarded with greed in old fishing stories, especially those in vogue in the 1930s, 1940s, and 1950s, the sort of John Taintor Foote–style of fishing tale where the not-quite-well-enough-off angler is at constant odds with his traditional, silly, and unsympathetic wife over the purchase of yet another vintage Spinoza.

I think it has to do with insecurity. Bamboo rods are a form of instant proof, evidence that we have arrived as fishermen.

Or maybe it's the security of knowing we've graduated, in financial status if not in skill, from the bargain-store, gaudy, anonymous tackle we started with. We are uneasy when approached by a fellow angler with a cheap glass rod, especially if it's yellow with green wraps and looks as thick as a mutant carrot as he waves it around in happy innocence. He reminds us of our former self. He *is* our former self, before we acquired Taste.

I understand that one of the bamboo-rod builders has noticed that, though they keep selling the rods at a steady clip, repairs have dropped off to nearly nothing. People are still buying them but aren't using them enough to break them anymore. Here we approach a consideration of the collecting mentality, which I have elsewhere compared to the medieval search for religious relics. Bamboo rods, along with all their other social attachments, are on their way to becoming pieces of the True Cross. That's a topic that makes even a cynical iconoclast like me nervous, so I'll let it go. I'm in enough trouble already, without offering a rumination on the psychology of artifact worship. What you do with your bamboo rod in the privacy of your own home is your business.

We fish for mood as we fish for trout. We should do it however we find it most fulfilling, whether we want to use tiny dry flies or streamers the size of chipmunks. If I were able to order a rod that would best suit my mood for a small stream I know not far from here, what I guess I'd really like is about a 7-foot, three-piece rod for a 4-weight line. The butt and midsections would be greenheart, perhaps varnished, perhaps impregnated like the Orvis bamboo rods. I would have my choice of five tips: two in lancewood for the slowest, softest casting, two in bamboo for a little more *umph*, and one in graphite, just in case. I would install a Hardy Featherweight reel on it, and on this reel I would put the darkest, most dignified line I could find. I would keep the whole thing in a leather case, getting it out a few times each season, just on sunny days when I could most enjoy the light on all that beautiful wood as it bends to greet each bright little trout that rises to my fly.

Nine

HENDRICKSONS

SPRING is a time of unbridled appetites. Everything, from winter-lean bears to sun-starved trees, is suddenly back in business with a vengeance, consuming, moving, and growing. Hunger drives animals to new feeding grounds, and it makes them incautious, even reckless. Trout, roused after months of iced-in lethargy, are at their most ravenous and least careful. The water is high and a little roily, which may increase their recklessness. It's a perfect time for Hendricksons.

The Hendrickson is a long-popular artificial fly that is most often associated with a group of mayflies named *Ephemerella subvaria*, *Ephemerella invaria*, and *Ephemerella rotunda*, one of the first major hatches throughout the East and Midwest. In some places the Hendrickson is preceded by the Quill Gordon or some lesser-known insect, but for many fishermen it is the true harbinger of the season's dry-fly fishing, which makes us love it even more.

Some of the best Hendrickson hatches I've seen have been on Michigan's Au Sable. Whether on the upper river near Grayling or many miles farther down, below the dam at Mio, the Hendricksons behaved pretty much the same. The fly has a reputation for gentlemanly hours, and it did not usually emerge until early afternoon; once it started, the emergence sometimes lasted only half an hour, sometimes for three hours or so, intermittently. Many writers have remarked how pleasant it is to sleep late, spend some time tying a few flies or fussing with gear, eat a leisurely lunch, and then wander down to the river to meet the hatch.

Fewer writers have remarked on what regular fishermen (that is, those who don't fish the perpetually sunny pages of books) all dread as "Hendrickson weather," but most of the comments I've heard about Hendrickson weather couldn't be printed in popular magazines anyway. Hendricksons may be the harbingers of spring, but they don't necessarily wait for it. And even if the weather is tolerably wretched, the flies might not emerge. This still doesn't make any sense to me—what possible evolutionary advantage an insect species could find in taking random days off in the middle of its mating season—but it is part of the perverse romance of fishing the Hendricksons.

Not that this was such a big problem for my brother Steve when we fished the Au Sable. His favorite fly-fishing ritual was Getting Ready, which he referred to as foreplay. Foreplay was all the time spent tying flies and leaders (I can't believe we actually used to bother to tie our own leaders), sorting out stuff in our vests, reading the books in which famous fishermen actually caught fish on Hendrickson imitations in balmy spring weather, sorting out stuff in our vests, hammering on the cabin's recalcitrant water pump, and sorting out stuff in our vests. Even then it was clear to me that Steve was well on his way to abandoning actual fishing entirely, so satisfying did he find all these preliminaries.

Which made him perfectly suited to the Hendrickson. He used to assure me that in a good week of this spring fishing you hoped for one or two days when the hatch actually happened. He seemed a little more pleased about this than I thought reasonable, but what with his enthusiasm for foreplay, I let it go. If the weather threatened to improve, we could always drive over to Grayling or Roscommon and cruise the tackle shops— buying stuff added zest to foreplay—until it was time to go out and stand in the cold rain and watch the insects refuse to emerge.

Hendrickson imitations are probably a good deal older than commonly imagined. Angling historian Austin Hogan believed that one of George Gibson's flies, tied 160 or more years ago for the Pennsylvania spring creeks, was an intentional Hendrickson imitation. No doubt other equally thoughtful fishermen also noticed the fly back then and tied up something to imitate it; it was too common an insect, and too obviously popular with the trout, to be ignored by savvy anglers. It wasn't until early in the twentieth century, though, that imitations of this hatch became widely publicized. In fact the fly didn't even get a name until 1918.

The fly pattern was originated by Roy Steenrod, now thought to have been the only man taught to tie flies by the great Catskill angler Theodore Gordon. Steenrod was himself an outstanding fly tier, and his own story of the fly's creation has come down to us in various versions.

Steenrod once told Harold Smedley, author of *Fly Patterns and Their Origins* (1943), that the fly was created to imitate a hatch he encountered on New York's Beaverkill in 1916. It didn't get named, according to this account, until two years later, when Steenrod was fishing that same river with A. E. Hendrickson, an executive at the United States Trucking Corporation and an enthusiastic angler. Steenrod told Smedley that "one day while sitting on the bank of the stream about two years after I had tied the first patterns, the matter was brought up as to what I would call or name the fly. Looking at A.E., the best friend a person could ever wish to have, I said 'the fly is the Hendrickson.' "

In another version, Steenrod wrote a letter to Catskill angler-entomologist Preston Jennings, telling Jennings that the fly was created in 1918. The letter, now part of the Jennings Collection at the American Museum of Fly Fishing, explained that "the Hendrickson Fly I first tied in 1918 and named it after A. E. Hendrickson my friend with whom I fish and shoot and have had many pleasant hours in his company." Steenrod eventually sent Jennings a sample of the fly, and years later that fly was given by Jennings's widow to Arnold Gingrich, who saw to it that the fly ended up in the museum.

The Hendrickson is normally tied on a size 12 or 14 hook. The body on the Steenrod original at the museum is a medium tan, almost straw colored. Both the tail and the wings are pale wood duck, and the hackles are medium dun. Sometimes Steenrod recommended using a few strands of golden pheasant crest for a tail; like Gordon, Steenrod was not inflexible about fly patterns and did a good deal of experimenting.

Even when it was young, the fly underwent some interesting permutations. By the late 1930s there was also a Dark Hendrickson, which substituted darker wood-duck flank feather for the wings and had a dark gray body about the same shade as the modern Adams. From then on it becomes difficult to tell exactly which of the two flies—the Light or Dark—many later fishing writers thought they were tying. The distinction has now disappeared from most commercial ties you'll see in fly shops and catalogues; most now seem to simply call the Light Hendrickson the Hendrickson; I suppose if you want a Dark Hendrickson, you might as well just admit you need an Adams.

But to a greater extent than almost any other dry-fly pattern, the Hendrickson underwent reinterpretation by many of the century's most important fly-fishing writers. One of the great treats of being in charge of the museum was getting a firsthand look at how the best fishing minds worked over the best flies. Edward Hewitt, whose expert opinions prevailed in a series of books before 1950, used dun hackle fibers for the tail, a change most modern tiers also agree on. Preston Jennings, writing in his milestone *A Book of Trout Flies* (1935), expressed devotion to the original Steenrod dressing, specifying wood-duck flank feathers for the tail, but he must have been open-minded about it, because all the Jennings Hendricksons at the museum use dun hackle fibers instead. (Jennings, incidentally, suggested that a popular wet fly in the old days, the Lady Beaverkill, may have been taken by the trout for drowned mayflies of the Hendrickson type.) Of later tier-authors, only Vermont's John Atherton seems to have stuck with golden pheasant crest for the tail. One or two of the

Atherton Hendricksons at the museum use the crest fibers, though Atherton obviously never stopped experimenting, even with the good patterns. Rummaging through the personal fly collection of someone like Jennings or Atherton is a good reminder that our lives are a lot more complicated than our public pronouncements; you see a lot of flies that could be based on a Hendrickson, or an Adams, or some other standard pattern, but you have no way of knowing whether the tier was consciously modifying a standard, or was just messing around and happened to approach one without quite getting it.

The Hendrickson pattern was at last standardized, probably permanently, in 1947, by Art Flick in his little *Streamside Guide*. To Mr. Flick goes the peculiar accolade of having turned the attention of thousands of later fly tiers to the search for urine-stained fur from the underbelly of a female red fox; the color of that fur was just the right shade, according to Flick, to match the body of the adult mayfly. Others had suggested this earlier, but it wasn't until Flick's affordable volume appeared that the idea caught on, and indeed there is a great deal to it. Most of the Hendricksons I've seen have a pinkish-olive cast that is almost indescribable as a color but is quite like the fur in question.

At the same time, you have to wonder who first noticed this and if it seemed as weird to his buddies as it seems to most people who hear about it today. "So, Bob, Ralph says he saw you cutting the crotch fur off a road-killed fox the other night; do we need to talk?"

Flick also popularized, indeed created, the modern Red Quill fly dressing that so many authors insisted is necessary to imitate the *male* of this group of mayflies, the Hendrickson dry fly being regarded as a good imitation only of the female.

Rarely are anglers called upon to use two different patterns to imitate the male and female of the same fly, but this was for a long time an accepted fashion when Hendricksons are hatching. I have to admit, the differences have never been obvious to me, but when I lived in Hendrickson country I dutifully carried both patterns for some years, partly out of insecurity and partly because the Red Quill is a beautiful fly too, though mine were only a scruffy insult to the perfection of Flick's originals.

Being able to see flies tied by these real masters is both inspiring and dismaying, and never was that combination of responses stronger than when I got my first good look at Flick's flies. Even as my eye for such things got better and better with experience, his dry flies always elicited a second look; my first reaction was always that nothing made in a fly-tying vise could be so perfect. The hackles appeared to come from some evolutionary advancement on the chicken theme, a bird that was on the verge of turning into something with stainless-steel feathers. The quill body tapered more evenly than it could have been drawn by a professional draftsman, much less tied by human hands. And of course the proportions were perfect. For a while I was lucky enough to have some beautiful Red Quills tied by Richard Kress, a New Jersey friend who had an uncanny feel for the proportions and style of the Flick fly, but they gradually migrated from my fly box by way of my leader to the vegetation of several Eastern streams.

Like many old fly patterns, the Hendrickson has undergone more radical modifications. It appeared at a time when a new dry-fly pattern automatically resulted in the tying of an equivalent wet fly, but there have been many other briefly prominent variations, and, I assume, countless local ones. Probably the most important and enduring modification was introduced by

Vincent Marinaro in *A Modern Dry Fly Code* (1950). Marinaro applied his "thorax" style of tying to the pattern, moving the wing back toward the middle of the body, reproportioning the fly to make it more realistic.

Though as a historian I am more susceptible than most to the charms of studying the evolution of a great fly pattern, I must admit that all this history has surprisingly little to do with whether or not you catch fish when the Hendricksons are hatching. After fishing the hatch in four states, and under a good many conditions, it gradually dawned on me that I was being taken for a ride by my historical preoccupation.

It should have been clear to me in Michigan more than twenty years ago, there on the Au Sable. Steve ties beautiful flies; every morning he would crank out a few delicate thorax duns *à la* Marinaro, while I'd clumsily mangle a few nondescript old materials into shape around a hook, producing flies so magnificently lumpy and unconvincing that my brother accused me of making them out of pocket lint from my jeans. He called them "thorax humpies."

But, wonder of wonders, I caught more fish than he did, almost every day. At the time I thought it was a fluke (he claimed the sun was in his eyes), but later, when I fished the Hendricksons for five years on the Battenkill, the lesson was reinforced. One unusually nice day (Vermont actually had these during the Hendricksons), I arrived on the river an hour or two early for the hatch. A woman of considerable interest was with me, and I was trying to impress her with my streamcraft, so of course I succeeded only in quickly losing all of my Hendricksons in nearby trees and weeds, every cast worse than the last. I even managed to break my fly line, something

I had never dreamed was possible. By the time the hatch started, I was so mortally embarrassed and ashamed that I was hoping I might just quietly slip beneath the surface of the river. Only the continued enthusiasm (for the fishing, not for me) of the woman caused me to root around in my fly boxes for any old thing that might work. Sure enough, any old thing I tried worked. The fish didn't care at all. I was beginning to catch on.

Asking around, I discovered that some of the best fishermen I knew remained loyal to the "official" Hendrickson imitation only because they liked how it looked. They cheerfully admitted that an Adams, or a Pheasant Tail, or any number of other flies, worked just as well. The mystery of the Pocket Lint Fly was solved. The fish really didn't care.

I heard now and then of days when only the perfectly tied Hendrickson, or a sparse, smoothly wrapped Red Quill will interest finicky trout. I'm sure such days occurred. I just didn't see very many of them. If Hendrickson-type mayflies hatched later in the summer, when the water was lower and clearer, they would probably require more precise imitations, but in the spring it isn't as critical. And so I suppose it would be smart to make sure you always have a few of the "correct" pattern on hand, either for emergency situations or in case the social occasion demands you use a proper Hendrickson.

The Hendrickson appears in late April and early May. There are extremes; it may appear earlier, and it may last throughout May. Ideally, you should go out in the morning, as early as you'd like after full light, and fish the nymph for a couple of hours. There are several popular Hendrickson nymphs; from a distance of more than a few inches they all look more or less alike, with medium-brown bodies on size 12 or 14 hooks. Catskill professional Art Lee, author of a truly authoritative book on dry-fly fishing, recommends starting as early as 7:00 A.M. and fishing two nymphs, casting them quartering downstream. Lee also suspects that there is a period of feeding inactivity when the fish won't take flies, just before the main hatch begins. This is the time most other authors say you should be fishing the nymph hardest, so the choice is yours.

The hatch usually starts, if it's going to, in the early afternoon. Depending on your time zone, it may be 1:00 or 2:00 P.M. or so. It may start before noon on occasion, but if you're out there dutifully flailing away with nymphs in the morning, you will catch it. There is a good chance of success with emerger patterns—sort of short-winged wet flies—just before and even during the main hatch; they've worked for me a few times and come highly recommended by most of the famous fishing authors. Doug Swisher and Carl Richards, in *Emergers* (1991), show some really helpful photographs of the behavior of emergers. But I notice that they also say that recent changes in weather have changed the rules about Hendricksons, at least temporarily; they're seeing hatches as early as 9:00 A.M. in Michigan. You will just have to ask locally to find out the hatching time in your area. The only personal contribution I can make to this lore is that I clearly recall watching Hendrickson nymphs in Michigan, in slow, clear water where I could see them almost from the moment they left the river bottom, and at least some of them swam up through the water nearly to the surface, then settled back toward the bottom, repeating this two or three times before actually breaking through the surface film and getting down to the business of breaking out of the shuck and unfolding their wings. One of the most powerful moments in my checkered career as a naturalist was holding a Hendrickson nymph on my fingertip while it split its shuck down the back, crawled out, and unpacked its accordioned wings.

The hatch itself is always a wonder, no matter how often I see it. Maybe it's because of the long winter that is just then past, but I doubt that I'm the only angler whose nerves get a little shaky when all those flies appear. After a winter of deprivation this sudden offering of good sport is strong stuff.

Luckily the Hendricksons don't often get so thick that your fly is lost in the crowd. I never saw an even moderately heavy hatch on the Battenkill, nothing to compare with the more numerous flies on the Au Sable. Usually there are enough flies to keep the fish interested in feeding and to provide intermittent activity for a good part of the afternoon. Later in the day, into early evening, spinners from the previous day's hatch fall to the water, and again the fish may rise. As with the rest of the day, the evening spinner fall is hard to predict; consulting local fishermen, or learning by your own experience, is the best way to know what to expect. Even then, don't expect it too confidently.

For me, uncertainty and surprise pretty much define the Hendricksons. When I think of that season and its fly hatches, one almost stereotypical Hendrickson day comes to mind. It was May 18, and Boston publisher David Godine and I were fishing Grand Lake Stream in Maine, a little way down from its famous hatchery. According to my fishing log, the weather was "alternating sunshine and hurricane." Snow squalls, carried straight downstream on a bitter wind, made it difficult to imagine any good fishing. We waded into the water about 1:30, Dave in his usual good cheer and I huddled crankily in my parka, slapping a big streamer out across an apparently fishless river. I was about to quit when the curtain of snow suddenly lifted and the sky cleared; the sun surprised us with its warmth.

As quickly, there were fish showing. The river came to life with dozens of rise forms as landlocked salmon materialized from some hidden shelters. What I at first thought were a few vagrant snowflakes proved to be large, pale mayflies. After a few clumsy grabs I caught one and recognized the general sort of springtime shape and color of the Hendrickson. I didn't know (or care) if they were the "true" *Ephemerella whatchamacalla* the Hendrickson was supposed to imitate. All I cared was that they appeared when Hendricksons should, and they looked like Hendricksons looked everywhere else I'd seen them. I called down to Dave to put on one of the Red Quills I'd given him that morning before we went out.

There followed twenty minutes of almost constant action. Few fish were actually landed, but the action was all we could want. Landlocked salmon are quick, and these seemed to fight themselves to exhaustion in only a couple of minutes. They were lean, 14 to 18 inches long, and spent most of their time in the air. One 16-incher actually tail-walked for about 8 feet across the surface, the first time I'd ever seen a freshwater fish do that. I heard occasional whoops from downstream as Dave hooked fish after fish.

Then the next wave of snow squalls hit us from the lake, and the rises stopped. We hunkered over in our parkas and shivered there in the water for a few minutes, but it passed and the rise was on again. After three or four such episodes, the rise stopped for good. It was about 3:00, and we had to be in Boston that night, but the nine-hour drive seemed a lot less dreadful after this great fishing.

I had noticed that Dave had been hooking fish as fast as I had, and so when we met on the bank, I waited impatiently for some word of compliment on my foresight at having the right flies ready. When it became clear he wasn't going to say anything about it, I asked for it: "Those Red Quills really worked great, huh, Dave?"

His response was slow in coming, almost sheepish. "Uh, yeah, I guess so. Actually I forgot to put 'em in my vest—left 'em on the dresser back at the cabin. But I did okay with this; it's a little beat up, but the fish liked it a lot." Thus deflating my balloon of triumph, he held up a fly that for all its chewed-up rattiness was instantly recognizable as that great pie-in-the-face of all hatch matchers, the Royal Coachman. About the same time, he admitted that he'd also forgotten his floating line and had fished the entire hatch with a high-density sink-tip line, which obliged him to make very short drifts because his dry fly would be dragged under the surface almost immediately. His whole performance was a perverse tribute to the traditional vicissitudes of Hendrickson fishing.

But I began by talking about unbridled appetites, and it was in fact the Hendrickson that put me in a position to meet the biggest such appetite I am likely to find on a trout stream, unless I finally make Yellowstone's Foremost Stupid Mistake and stumble upon a grizzly bear while fishing. I was again in Michigan, where Steve and I were on the Au Sable, several miles downstream from Mio. This is big water, and we were working the edge of a long pool that stretched downstream into an immense hole that we assumed was bottomless; it looked like you could sink a bus in it. There were quite a few small trout rising, and both of us were hooking a few fish on our respective Hendrickson interpretations.

I picked out a steady riser, missed it, and then a few casts later hooked it solidly. As Steve and I watched, the fish jumped twice. It was pretty small, but in those days I displayed an unseemly pride every time I had a fish on when Steve didn't, and I was planning how to milk the situation for as much as I could when the fish suddenly changed tactics. It dove and headed downstream, and even my inexperienced reflexes were sharp enough to recognize serious power. I let it run. My 4X tippet would not have turned a fish with this much strength.

As I waded downstream after the fish, I passed Steve and made some remark about him picking me up later at McKinley Bridge, a few miles downstream. He expressed surprise, and with more than a little superiority told me that such a small fish shouldn't be played so lightly. He was unable to feel the insistent pressure I was feeling in the line, though, so I hurried on.

The fish stopped maybe 100 feet downstream from him. I was near the bottomless hole now, and the river was only wadable a few yards out from the bank. The bottom was covered with tree branches, the bank was steep, and I could not easily climb out of the water to try to get below the fish, the way all the books say you're supposed to. I abandoned my pride and asked Steve if he would bring his net and help me. Little brook trout just never had acted like this before.

Annoyed and impatient at having to leave rising fish, he sloshed out of the water and stalked down the bank. When he got even with where I thought the fish was holding, he squinted at the murky water for a minute thoughtfully, then frowned. "There's something funny about its mouth . . . it's . . . Holy Ford!" (Living so near Detroit, Steve is fascinated by cars and frequently employs colorful automotive expressions in his conversation.)

In a rapid stream of car talk, he explained that my little brook trout was now crosswise in the mouth of a giant brown trout. At first, looking for a small brook trout, his eyes did not admit the existence of more, but then suddenly the big fish came into focus. Spots like Falcon quarters, for Chrysler's sake, he yelled, and so on. One of the river's Mother Trout had risen out of the big hole and was feeding on the little risers. My little brook trout, acting wacky because it was hooked, had attracted the attention of this monster.

This was artificials-only water, and bait fishing (I *think* that's what I was doing right then) was of course illegal. There was little question, in ethical terms, of what I should do: I should pull my line free, whether I lost the fly, the small trout, or whatever. So of course, with no hesitation, we decided to try like hell to kill this big mother. After some frantic discussion, Steve slipped into the water below the fish, which was hanging there on my line, the only calm participant in this drama. Very slowly, I reeled in enough line so that I too could see the long, broad shape of the fish maybe 15 feet downstream from me. It was somewhere between 25 and 30 inches long, I suppose, but its mass, rather than its length, was what gave us both the shakes. This was a trout with shoulders.

I assumed that, not feeling any hook, the big brown wasn't spooked or frightened, but I couldn't imagine what it made of a little brook trout that could tow it upstream like that without moving a fin. The plan, as it developed, was that Steve would wade up behind the big trout and do something unimaginable but spectacular with his tiny net. By now we were both pushing our automotive vocabularies to the limit as we shuffled around, gawking at this enormous fish. It was obviously aware of us and would swing out into the deeper current whenever

Steve approached it. It occurred to us that I might be able to suddenly release pressure on the line, causing the big fish to drift unaware back into Steve's clutches, but the big trout was too smart for that, and after a couple of minutes of listening to us strategize, it finally just let go. As the brookie came free, the bend in my rod straightened, and the little fish skittered over the surface toward me. The brown made one last dash at it then, but turned away before getting very close to me. As we stood there, momentarily stunned by the whole event, the big trout drifted out toward the middle of the river and then sank down until it faded from sight.

I reeled in the little fish, which was still alive but suffered from massive internal and external injuries. Its eyes bulged out, either from internal pressure or from raw fear. I measured it at 9 1/2 inches, and because it was not a legal fish, dutifully returned it to the water.

The big fish dominated our conversations the rest of the trip. Steve's childhood training on Ohio carp waters came to the surface. "What we *shoulda* done was give him lots of slack. Then he would have taken the brookie down into the hole and swallowed it. Then, if we'd waited long enough, you might have been able to set the hook in his gut." I was skeptical—the leader was only 4X, after all, and it must take hours, if not days, for a whole brook trout to be digested—but it was an intriguing thought.

I had an even more intriguing thought. I immediately tied up my first original fly pattern, which I christened The Nine-Inch Brook Trout. The fly was really only about 5 inches long—a sort of mutant Lefty's Deceiver, with long, brown-dyed grizzly saddle hackles and an extra hook or two hanging out the rear end—but it seemed just the thing for that once-in-a-life-time occasion when a huge fish comes up and takes a fish you're playing, an occasion I, of course, had already had once in my lifetime. I carried the fly around for a few years, and even had a memorable hit on it in Vermont once, but finally it vanished, the way flies seem to do after a while.

A few weeks after the Michigan trip, I returned to my summer work in Yellowstone and got up the nerve to tell someone about the big trout. The first person I told was a local guide, who listened with that glassy-eyed politeness they're so good at. A few weeks later I ran into him again, and he was kind of excited. "You know, when you told me about that big fish eating a little fish you were playing, I guess I didn't really believe you, but just the other day the very same thing happened to me on the Firehole. It was amazing." He didn't land his big fish either, but it didn't matter to me. I believed him.

I also believed my brother, who said the same thing had happened to him (in the same lifetime!) at least four other times on the Au Sable's bigger water, and who assured me it was a common practice among the most predatory local fishermen to fish at night with "crude, giant muddlerlike things . . . these guys put meat on the table, and they don't read books about it."

I've since met or read about a few other people who have had the same experience. Over the years, a few iconoclastic writers have suggested that, even during a heavy hatch, you might catch more fish with a nymph. One or two have even recommended fishing a streamer, because all those small fish, out feeding in the open like that, constitute a sort of secondary hatch of their own, and once in a while, maybe only once in a lifetime, a well-placed streamer might strike the fancy of one of those mobile sections of river bottom that no longer even feel an urge to reach their nose through the surface film and sip down a floating fly. I have often wondered, were I to return to

Hendrickson streams now and live with them for a few years, if I might just switch over to streamers each spring. It wouldn't be dry-fly fishing, but it would still depend entirely on the hatch, so in some remote, optimistic way I could still claim that I was fishing to the Hendricksons.

Ten

CIVILIZED FISHING

I WAS making my way up a forested stretch of the Battenkill just below Manchester one evening, when I encountered a fly fisherman coming the other way. He told me he'd seen a large fish under a fallen log upstream but had been unable to catch it. I immediately recognized the log (and the fish) as my own goal for the evening. I'd been watching that fish, or at least imagining its presence, for weeks. A few nights earlier, a streamer I'd managed to work back under the log had been wrenched momentarily from its swing, the closest I ever came to catching one of the Battenkill's really big trout.

I was annoyed at this fellow, knowing he had probably spooked the fish, and knowing also that the only real chance to catch it was still an hour ahead of us, in the dark of early night. But I remember something about that encounter much more clearly than my disappointment. When he described the fish and its hiding place, he gave himself away as a New Yorker, up to Vermont for the weekend, by saying that the spot was "about a block upstream from here." Applying the measure of urban geography to a trout stream was so monstrously incongruous that I instantly despised the guy.

Angling historian Kenneth Cameron has pointed out how much unlike our ancestors we modern anglers are. Two hundred years ago the good fly fishermen, or most of them, learned their stream lore from the stream; they lived along it, and what they knew about it was the result of experience. They also learned, directly, from fellow anglers, many from family members whose lore had passed through several generations. Now, most of what we know we learn less directly—from books, videos, classes, guides, club meetings, and so on. Two hundred years ago the many booming fishing schools of today would have been unimaginable, to say nothing of unnecessary. Only a few very wealthy people were able to "get away for the weekend" to fish their favorite stream. Hardly any of us live within walking distance of the waters we fish. We are urban, and modern transportation makes us think of places hundreds of miles away as if they were in our backyard.

In the years I've been fly fishing, I've been lucky enough to be more or less a "local" rather than a city fisherman. In several places, I've lived within a mile or so of the trout stream I fished, in one case even having trout within a hundred feet of my front door. Because of that, I suppose, I was inclined to adopt the sometimes jealous, even selfish, perspective of the local person who comes to dislike city fishermen.

It wasn't hard to dislike them, I must admit. I'd see famous outdoor writers who lived in New York or New Jersey or some other unfathomably unpleasant place carefully plan their annual trip to "my" river, making a few expensive phone calls just so they could hit the peak of the hatch they wanted; they'd do that year after year, of course, but almost as soon as their plane landed back at La Guardia Airport after their first trip they were writing about it like old hands, paraphrasing what their guides told them, fulfilling their roles as experts before flying off to some other faraway water to become an expert on it too. They, I muttered, pretended to know the rivers I fished, but they never gave them a thought in February, when I saw them deep in ice, or in November, when the eagles gathered in the cottonwoods. Their acquaintance with them was a one-night stand, a cheap thrill. They picked the best time to catch the most fish and get the most enviable story, and I didn't mind knowing how often the river foiled them with sulking trout or sudden high water.

As fly-fishing has become more popular, I think more local fishermen share this suspicion of visitors. In *The Habit of Rivers* (1994), Ted Leeson justifies that suspicion as well as I've seen:

> On Friday, a Boston neurosurgeon is standing stark naked in a fly shop, wielding a fistful of major credit cards. On Saturday, he's fully outfitted in the front of a driftboat being rowed down the Green or the Bighorn, catching the biggest trout he may ever see in his life. It isn't some gunnysack mentality that's worrisome. This guy probably enjoys the experience of being outdoors and appreciates the beauty of rivers as much as anyone. Tackle dealers and guides love him. But to the long-time fisherman, inveterate tinkerer, catcher of bugs, and tyer of flies, there is a hole in the middle of the neurosurgeon's sport that threatens to transform fly fishing. The approach seems antiseptic, too few hands laid on too few things to satisfy a fisherman's desire for wholeness.

There's a whole bundle of complaints here, all of which are important, and Ted is talking about the beginning fisherman, stereotyped as "getting into fly-fishing" because of its sudden fashionableness. I'm talking more specifically about fishermen of any length of experience who don't have a river of their own, by which I mean a river close by that is essentially their home stream. Because they are visitors to the rivers they fish only occasionally, even if they fish them very well, I wonder how they can have enough "hands-on" wholeness in their fishing life, which, I suppose, leads me to doubt their seriousness, even their sincerity. But I know that's not especially clear thinking on my part.

In the 1970s, when I occasionally joined my brother Steve to fish in Michigan, we participated in what he called The Parade: thousands of urbanites fleeing northward from Detroit for a few frantic hours of relaxation in the sticks. It was bumper-to-bumper on the interstate by the time we got to Flint, then gradually the flow eased as weekend warriors peeled off to various little towns and lakes north of there.

At the time, I lived in Wyoming and was smug about it. "Boy, you know, I just couldn't live like this, so far from the fishing." Steve would mumble something about living where one could find the work one wanted, and I'd shrug and forget it. But knowing that my brother was a city fisherman made this whole business of disliking them a little more complicated. After all, he got me started at fly-fishing, and he seemed to have all the right attitudes and intentions; maybe the others were okay too.

Of course they were; at least they were no worse, on the average, than the local fishermen. In my own travels, I've often discovered that it's the locals who have the least appreciation for what they have, whether it's a salmon river or a trout stream. It's been there as long as they can remember, and getting to it isn't something they look forward to fifty weeks of the year. They take it for granted. Most of the rivers I've fished a lot owe most of their present health to the interest and energy of city fishermen who get together and force lawmakers to pay attention to good resource management. Having so little good fishing out their back door, city fishermen come to value it that much more highly.

But even as I overcame the worst of my resentments I realized that there were perceptible differences between the average city fisherman and the average local. For example, there's crowd tolerance. I've often wondered if the packed-in fishermen who flail away over the cutthroats at Buffalo Ford on the Yellowstone River in Yellowstone Park were interviewed what percentage of them would be city fishermen. For a while in the 1970s and 1980s, Buffalo Ford was near the top of the name-dropping list at the Eastern fly-fishing soirees I attended (some of these people actually thought it was the name of the river), but most locals I know didn't go near the place because it was so crowded. There are plenty of fish to go around, but who needs the crowds?

On the other hand, I don't suppose the average Manhattan-based fisherman, accustomed to much worse crowds on most Catskill waters, minds all those people so close. He probably even enjoys it, or just figures it's the way things have to be. He's used to sidewalks that are more crowded still, every day, going to work. I'm not, and so I resent it, here in the West, when some tourist passes by miles of empty stream just so he can wallow into the water 30 feet upstream from me and offer a neighborly greeting. Some of these guys seem to *need* the company.

Others need some stern advice. Miss Manners has it that

manners are the only thing that keep us from killing each other. Lack of manners is certainly the foremost problem on modern trout streams. A few years ago I was fishing the Yellowstone River in the park, right along the road just upstream from the Otter Creek bridge. I had located a tight, elongated pod of rising trout along 6 or 8 feet of the bank, and I was casting to them from below, putting a dry fly over the whole pod, hoping for a take from any one of them. I was vaguely aware of a man getting out of his car across the road, a man who engaged my Stereotype Radar by his perfect newness. He was what I would later come to think of as a cookie-cutter fly fisherman, as I saw small packs of them descend from shiny new Suburbans, all matching each other in acres of well-pressed L. L. Bean khaki and stone-washed denim. He geared up, standing there by his Jeep/Bronco/Suburban, then hurried across the road, at which point he noticed my fish.

Make no mistake about this; by any decent sporting code, they *were* mine. By any modern standard, and by practically all older standards, I had irrevocable claim to the narrow lane of water I was draping my fly line over, and to the fish in it, until I chose to leave. So I was more shocked than angry when this man hurried to a point perhaps 20 feet above the fish and began casting down to them, covering the same water as my fly was just then covering.

It would be the easy way out to characterize this man as a classic aggressive urban overachiever whose rat-maze existence had led him to a life of hasty greed. But at my calmest I know he was just ignorant. Bud Lilly, who in more than sixty years of fly-fishing has seen a stunning array of such bad behavior, says that the well-heeled modern who decides to get into fly-fishing seems to presume that he's buying good judgment and manners when he buys his tackle.

All facets of society have codes of behavior, of common courtesy. This same man, were he to enter some other unfamiliar social arena, would hesitate until he figured out the ground rules. Whether he was at a bullfight or a bar mitzvah, he would look around to get some clues on how to act. So why does he behave like such a pig on the stream? Is it because, as a correspondent of mine has so sharply put it, fly-fishing attracts more egregious assholes than any other sport? It's sometimes tempting to think so, but I doubt that fly-fishing can outdo deer hunting, or bowling, or a lot of other sports in that category.

Perhaps it's just because fly-fishing's code of behavior, though it is as subtle and complex as that of many other pursuits, applies in such unfamiliar surroundings. The vast number of new fly fishers do seem to be urban or suburban: people intimately familiar with all kinds of restrictions and boundaries they must acknowledge just to maneuver through densely populated settings every day. A trout stream must seem entirely free of all that: no curbs, no meters running, no refs, no stoplights. There's a fish—it must be mine!

All this leads me two places. The first is to out-of-the-way places to fish, places I'm reasonably sure I'll encounter fewer fishermen. Luckily I can still find places like that. The second place isn't really a place so much as an attitude—a renewed attempt to tolerate people who have a different perspective on trout fishing than I do. The city fisherman has very little time; he doesn't have the chance to see the river all year long and may not be interested in doing so. I can sympathize with his haste in wanting the best fishing he can get. When I was in my twenties, working as a ranger-naturalist in Yellowstone, I was occasionally approached by a fisherman wanting some advice on where to get a good fishing guide. One day, after suggesting a couple of people, my curiosity overcame me and I told a fellow that I couldn't imagine hiring someone to show me where to fish; it seemed like cheating or something. For some reason he was kind and polite enough to remind me that I lived in the middle of the best trout fishing and had lots of time to get to know the good places. He, on the other hand, only had a week and really didn't want to spend it wandering around in ignorance. It still didn't sound quite right, but I recognized the sense of it.

So the city fisherman has his side to the story, no matter how annoyed I get to find his rental car parked at my favorite spot (or worse, his guide's Wagoneer parked there; somehow commerce makes it even more painful). I can also recognize my own vulnerability to criticism, because I am not really a local. I'm not a native along any stream I fish now; I'm just a transplanted city fisherman who has for quite a few years arranged to live along the rivers rather than just make hurried trips to them now and then.

And thank heaven the city fishermen are content to live in cities. I'm reminded of the idealistic wilderness enthusiasts who believe that if only everyone could have their wonderful experiences in the backcountry, then everyone would work to protect wilderness. If everyone even tried to have those experiences, wilderness would expire under the weight. It's like that in trout fishing; I must ask myself what it is that I *expect* from city fishermen. In order for them to think the way I do, they'd all have to live along the rivers like I do. The rivers couldn't stand that any more than I could, and so, though I may not always like the way they act, I couldn't be happier that they continue to be city fishermen. Having them around all the time would be infinitely worse.

As the years passed and I became more familiar with the joys of comfortable lodgings, smart guides, and other amenities denied an impoverished seasonal ranger, I also recognized that at least some of the time, civilized fishing of the sort these city fishermen preferred was a good thing. It could just have been that my tastes were adjusting to my income, or it could have been that I was slowing down and getting a little lazy, but I think it was also because I was getting a little smarter too. As a product of the 1960s, I will probably always retain a residual suspicion of anything very exclusive, but again and again since I turned forty, some wild place has been more memorable and more enjoyable because it was also pretty posh; there are plenty of places where I hope it never happens, but now and then I'm just as glad to see that we've brought some of the city with us to our favorite fishing spots.

The codes of behavior by which we define what is acceptable in fishing in fact require a great deal of flexibility of us. Fishing is what we make of it and what we decide, in each location, is best. We may change our minds in a few years, but at any given time the variation in definitions from place to place are profound. Frederick Halford, fishing his private, expensive, and manicured chalkstreams (American anglers are startled to discover that chalkstream riverkeepers even trim the water weeds), was fishing the right way, just as I am when I slap a rubber-legged deer-hair bug down on a wilderness pool 10 miles from the nearest road. As impatient as I may get with the fishermen who come to "my" rivers with different attitudes and tolerances, I have to admit that this persistence of local tradition is one of the most attractive things about fly-fishing, and that the places that most preserve their own way of doing things are among my very favorites to fish.

The ancient, weatherworn mountains of northern New

York are home to one of America's oldest and best-kept angling traditions. Among sportsmen, the Adirondacks enjoyed a glory in the years following the Civil War that compared favorably with the fame earned by the Catskills in the early 1900s and by the Rockies in the 1970s. A century ago, ably celebrated by George Dawson, William Boardman, Richard Sherman, and a host of other sadly forgotten writers, the Adirondacks became one of America's foremost angling regions. And, like the other regions of later fame, the Adirondacks produced a regional fishing ethic and practice that will probably never completely vanish. Spectacular, brilliant wet flies, many originating locally and named for local waters and guides, were cast from elegant boats that are still known for their peculiar combination of delicate grace and sturdiness.

Despite a few well-known rivers, it was and still is primarily a still-water tradition. There are hundreds of lakes in the Adirondacks, and even today, in the face of viciously acidic precipitation, it is sometimes possible to enjoy fishing much like that encountered a hundred years ago. Even if the fishing is not always as fast, or the fish as large, as back then, there are other compensations to be had by participating in this quiet, almost stately form of the sport.

My first acquaintance with Adirondack fishing was years ago, when on a hasty drive through the mountains I stopped long enough to take a few small stocked fish from a well-known stream. But more recently I was fortunate enough to fish the old Adirondacks in a privately owned and superbly preserved setting where scientific research and progressive management have restored the vigor of the fisheries to an almost unbelievable extent. The people who were my hosts know who they are, who they were, and what they want from their fishing.

It was not, at first glance, my kind of fishing. More than a century ago, a local angler had described the technique my hosts used in *The American Angler*. It was known as "shoal fishing."

> The first fishing of the season occurs about the second week in May, a few days after the ice leaves the lake. Then the fish come up from deep water to the sandy shoals in pursuit of dace which is their main food at that season. They are not partial to the artificial fly, nor to the angle worm, though occasionally one is taken with the fly. The lure of this kind that is most successful is a slate-olive fly resembling the caddis fly, and this they are more likely to take when [it is] trolled a few feet under the water, than when cast and drawn on the surface.

Trolling wet flies has a long and honorable heritage, especially in the Northeast. It never sounded especially exciting to me. Only the flies seemed appealing. At the museum I had often admired the long, fluttery trolling flies tied by Charles Zibeon Southard, an amazingly opinionated and pompous fishing writer who flourished in the 1920s. His long, slightly tapered patterns seemed almost able to flutter of their own accord and must have been spookily alive in the water. But I'd done very little of this kind of fishing, and so I was unprepared for the satisfactions it provided.

Besides, the fish in question were lake trout, 15 to 20 inches long, and my only acquaintance with them was through hearsay from friends who described dragging big ones from cold Western lakes as being "like reeling in a log." I prided myself on being open-minded about the rights of fish to act pretty much the way they wanted, but I had written off lake trout as dogs, and so I was unprepared there too.

And I must say that for all the pleasure of the fishing itself, it is the setting I now remember most warmly. The lakeshore, where it was not lined by solid forest, was dotted with the "camps" of those lucky enough to have permanent access there. The camps were often rustic mansions, with attached boathouses whose carpeted ramps sloped easily into the water. I guess I wasn't really prepared for the luxury of it all, either, but I don't mind admitting that it was easy to adjust to that as well. Here also I was confronted with yet another complication in my distrust of city fishermen. Virtually none of these fishermen were local residents, but this was truly and exclusively their water. Only one I knew really lived here full time; the rest had homes in cities at least a few hours away and only visited their camps on weekends or for a summer vacation. In this permutation of the contrast between the city fisherman versus the local, they were somehow both. Civilization, even that part of it that encompasses angling society, is not simple.

The shallows frequented by the fish occurred along a mile or so of shoreline, and each evening anywhere from two to a dozen boats (these too were a splendid, beautifully constructed part of the tradition) would slowly drift back and forth, each trailing a pair of fly lines, working the good water for 100 yards out from shore.

The fishermen ate a reasonably early dinner and slid their boats into the water just at dusk, perhaps a little earlier if it was raining. There was plenty of room, though some experienced fishermen tried, as inconspicuously as possible, to make sure they rowed over certain spots as often as they could, spots that would be undistinguished to a visitor but that had some local reputation: just off the pier, just opposite that tree or this camp, where memory called up some earlier evening's triumphs.

It was a quietly social time. As the boats passed within conversational range of one another, brief exchanges took place, truncated little talks and debates that might continue, in brief installments, as the evening passed and the fishermen met again and again in the settling dark. Everybody wanted to catch fish, but enough could count on doing so that only one or two fishermen—not regulars but guests still ridden by city strains—exhibited any impatience or surliness. This was civilized fishing.

It also was easy fishing, at least at first glance. Not in that anybody caught a lot of fish fast, but in that there was very little to do, and what little had to be done was apparently pretty simple. We used full sinking fly lines, 6 and 7 weight, and fairly heavy leaders with large nymphs and standard streamer patterns; I caught my fish on a white Muddler Minnow.

For a while it seemed almost potluck who would get a hit. Every so often there'd be a whoop or a grunt or just a quiet rustling in a boat, as a bent rod pointed 20 or 30 yards astern to where a fish struggled. Even the pace of the action was serene and understated. Then I began to notice that some fishermen—the ones who were known to be good at other fishing—seemed to get the most hookups and, besides that, seemed most able to fight the trout all the way to the boat. I finally realized that, like all other forms of fishing, luck would do you good on the occasional night, but skill was what you wanted for regular results.

I also realized that, as is so often the case, skill was not easily defined or taught. What possible difference there could be in the many trailing flies, all the same patterns, all moving at the same speed and depth, that allowed some fishermen to catch so many while others caught so few, never did become clear, but I'd seen this sort of thing happen in other places. Some people are just better at it.

Shoal fishing added one more dimension to my personal portrait of American trout fishing. Here, as the rest of the country busied itself with polypropylene, graphite, and the latest fads in fly patterns and lines and reels, fishing hadn't changed, nor had the slightest reason to change, in more than a hundred years. They had it right. Why mess with it?

It was a fishing with its own justifiable pace, a comforting exercise to the accompaniment of dripping oars, intermittent laughter, and the soft shuffling of feet and pants along the ribs of the boat. The early spring chill was shaken off by the occasional strike and consequent furious reeling. As often as not the fish twisted free long before I got it to the boat. But I didn't find much to worry about in that, perhaps because my host was one of those with the mystical skill, and so I could count on at least getting to watch him do it right.

My last evening I was foolishly slow over dinner, and when I got to the boathouse it was all but dark and my host was gone, as we'd agreed he should be if I was delayed. He'd thoughtfully slid a small boat almost to the water's edge, with a rod rigged and ready in it, so I made a wobbly launch and was instantly adrift in a heavy mist; no sky, no water, just windless mist and the muffled soothing night noises of the northern forest.

As the shoreline receded behind me, the trees and camps faded from sight, and all I could see in that direction was the diffuse yellow glow of the occasional porch light or boathouse lantern spaced along the shore. I let out the whole fly line and rowed slowly out to the fishing lanes—or where I imagined the fishing lanes to be—hoping not so much to catch a fish as to avoid ramming anybody in this vibrant fog.

I shouldn't have worried. Few fishermen were out. I did at one point approach my host's boat close enough to exchange a few words, but as I recall we talked more about the surreal mood than about the fishing. It was like rowing in clouds, with Chinese lanterns, suspended from God knew what, glowing faintly in the distance.

I hooked no fish that night. I didn't even stay out very long. There was no danger of getting lost in the mist, but there were some social obligations coming up later in the evening, and after less than an hour of floating alone, my senses were pretty well saturated with the reverential calm of the fogged-in lake. So, squinting as I located the light on my host's boathouse, I slowly brought the boat around, and towed my fly line from the shoals and back to shore.

Eleven

OCCASIONS FOR HOPE IN THE HOOK AND BULLET PRESS

A VETERAN outdoor writer once explained to me the formula for a successful hunting or fishing story: "First you tell 'em what you're going to say, then you say it, then you tell 'em what you said." At the time I didn't know that this was common advice in many kinds of writing, but I immediately recognized it as the form of most outdoor stories, and I appreciated what it said about the general state of outdoor writing.

What is called outdoor writing is not simply writing on the outdoors. It usually involves fishing or hunting, and though it frequently overlaps with less consumptive pastimes, it is a distinct national writing form. It is distinguished from nature writing (where the writer hardly ever kills anything) and from environmental writing (where the writer hardly ever has any fun) and is widely regarded as a lower form of written expression, sort of what "jockspeak" ("Okay you guys, pair off by threes!") is to regular speech. For those who encounter it accidentally in a dentist's office or on an airplane, it seems an odd mixture of corny rhetoric ("I hauled back on the pole and gouged that big stainless steel hook into a fat old sow bronzeback") and Mark Trail commitment to frontier virtues that were long ago discarded by urban America. Outdoor writers seem to be more a figment of their readers'—and their publishers'—imaginations than are, say, pet or photography writers.

What would most surprise the uninitiated is the extent to which outdoor writing is viewed by its practitioners as Literature. Though outdoor writers know that they are part of the "hook and bullet press," they often operate in a self-important atmosphere where one is likely to hear enthusiastic references to "angling literature" as if it were a major literary form. In *My Moby Dick,* the novelist William Humphrey, who occasionally writes on sporting topics, described his first exploration of the fishing manuals:

> The angler had metamorphosed into the ichthyologist, and the prevailing prose reflected the change—if mud can be said to reflect. I found myself correcting it as I had done freshman themes in my years as a professor. You had to hack your way through it as through a thicket. Participles dangled, person and number got separated and lost, clichés were rank, thesauritis and sesquipedalianism ran rampant, and the rare unsplit infinitive seemed out of place, a rose among nettles. Yet, instead of weeding their gardens, these writers endeavored to grow exotics in them: orchids, passionflowers. Inside each of them was imprisoned a poet, like the prince inside the toad. What came

out was a richness of embarrassments: shoddy prose patched with purple—beautifully written without first being well written.

And yet it was William Humphrey who back in the 1970s brought the attention of the angling *literati* to an obscure, neglected masterpiece of angling literature, *Thy Rod and Thy Creel*, written by Pulitzer Prize–winning biographer and poet Odell Shepard in 1930. Humphrey, like Shepard, knew that the world of angling literature is a great deal smaller than the world of fishing writing and that we need to keep track of what little good stuff we have.

It is safe to say that without Izaak Walton, Shepard, and a light handful of others (including Humphrey), today's fishing writers would be a lot less inclined to puff up about the classiness of their craft. It has been the occasional gifted writer, or the infrequent guest appearance of some major literary or historical figure (whether it was Washington Irving, Henry Ward Beecher, Zane Grey, or Ernest Hemingway did not matter as much as that it was someone of great fame), that has done so much for the tone and self-respect of modern outdoor writing. From the beginning, the American outdoor-writing tradition has built itself upon an uneven combination of rare brilliant contributions and a massive production of worse.

In the early national period, sporting writers suffered the same cultural insecurities that burdened the better-known genres: They were in the deep shadow of their British forebears, and they were often reminded of it. Sydney Smith's famous taunt, "In the four quarters of the globe, who reads an American book?" was echoed by a British angling book, *The Angler's Souvenir* (1835), in an exchange between two British anglers:

Simpson: Have you ever seen any American books on angling, Fisher?

Fisher: No. I do not think there are any published. Brother
Jonathan is not yet sufficiently civilized to produce anything
original on the gentle art.

But Brother Jonathan was sufficiently sophisticated to be
stung by that accusation and had by that time made a modest
start in his own sporting civilization. As I mentioned earlier,
America's first sporting periodical, *The American Turf Register
and Sporting Magazine*, appeared in 1829, and the first important books followed in the 1840s and 1850s, most heavily derivative of British titles; they borrowed freely of technical
information, natural history, and sporting codes. Engravings
from British books were taken with only slight alterations, perhaps replacing a distant castle with a colonial mansion, or a
red deer stag with a white-tailed buck. Having sporting books
published in America was not the same as having American
sporting books.

No one better symbolizes the mixture of old and new that
characterized the early Victorian outdoor writer in America
than Henry William Herbert, perhaps the most popular American sporting writer before the Civil War. Herbert was born in
England, educated at Eton and Cambridge, and came to this
country in 1831. Reputed to be an established classical scholar,
his greatest ambitions lay in romance novels, of which he
wrote many. So worried was he about being labeled a sporting
writer that he wrote for the periodicals and published his many
successful outdoor books under the pseudonym of Frank
Forester.

The books, such as *Frank Forester's Fish and Fishing of the
United States and British Provinces of North America* (1849), *The*

Warwick Woodlands (1845), and *Frank Forester's Field Sports of the United States and British Provinces of North America* (1849), were immensely popular and gave him the lasting fame he never earned from his novels. His learning in British sporting traditions was unmatched in the New World; he appealed to many for the irresistible "tone" he gave to America's culturally embarrassed outdoor sports; and he was an ardent preacher of gentlemanly ethics at a time when the field was largely ruled by game hogs. Besides his powerful influence on matters of ethics and style (both literary and personal), he placed a permanent stamp on American sporting writing by fathering a separate tradition, that of sporting fiction.

Herbert, who died a suicide in 1858, did not outlive the transitional period during which Americans found their own way, largely independent of European writing. By the 1870s (and thanks more to a flourishing periodical press than to books) America had its own native sporting celebrity-authors whose writings were followed by an increasingly self-aware body of sportsmen.

Thaddeus Norris became known as the American Walton for his huge *The American Angler's Book* (1864), which not only encompassed all the fishing opportunities and techniques from the Gulf of Mexico to Canada, but contained engaging and enduring essays on the worth of sport. Its companionable tone made "Uncle Thad" the best-loved fishing writer of the nineteenth century; in a rumination on pipe smoking as having been "instituted expressly for the fisherman," Norris exclaimed, "What a pity it is that infants are not taught to smoke!" Theodore Van Dyke produced the durable *The Still Hunter* (1883), still arguably one of the best introductory books on deer hunting in American history. Robert Barnwell Roosevelt, at various times ambassador to the Netherlands,

New York congressman, novelist, and New York State Fish Commissioner (and at all times one of the most scandalously colorful characters in New York society), wrote with rare intelligence on both hunting and fishing and represented a now-lost crossover talent in outdoor writing. Before 1900, when wildlife science and management were embryonic in this country, it was possible to be a leading figure in both the popular and the technical literature; Roosevelt was such a figure.

The path from Forester's aristocratic manner and international ambivalence to something wholly American leads inevitably, and one might even say conclusively, to that most self-assured of Americans, Theodore Roosevelt. His output of books on hunting and wilderness adventure in the thirty years following 1885 would have been extraordinary for a full-time outdoor writer but were only one of many equally absorbing pursuits. Through his books he had an influence on the course of American outdoor writing that was never surpassed by any later writer. From his eminence as a leading citizen and political figure, from his perspective as one of the most gifted naturalists of his day, and from his personal creed wherein an active outdoor life was not only great fun but patriotic obligation (a sort of training for war), came a complete code for the conduct of sport and for the process of outdoor writing. Acknowledging that "there does not exist a more dismal species of literature than the ordinary cheap sporting volume," and that "it is a good thing to write books, but it is a better thing still to do the deeds which are worth being written about," Roosevelt filled his books with sermons about good writing as a part of good sport. He appreciated the start that Forester had made in establishing an American outdoor-writing tradition, but concluded that "unfortunately, he was a true cockney, who cared little for really wild sports, and he was afflicted with that dreadful pedantry which pays more heed to ceremonial and terminology than it does to the thing itself." For Roosevelt, "wild sports" were those that required greater hardiness than did grouse shooting, and "the thing itself" was more important than British preoccupations with proper sporting attire and other social conventions.

Theodore Roosevelt occupies a position in outdoor writing much like that occupied by John Muir in nature writing. Both were powerful, formative characters who popularized creeds— they did not so much originate them as codify a lot of ideas drifting loose at the time and give the code the stamp of their own unique personalities. Both wrote prose sermons, though for different congregations. And both were set on pedestals by subsequent generations of writers in their respective fields.

Roosevelt was a kind of prototype, or role model, for the mainstream of outdoor writing since his time. By the time of his death in 1919, the form of modern outdoor writing, especially in books, was firm. His books, such as *The Wilderness Hunter* (1893) and *Outdoor Pastimes of an American Hunter* (1905), are lessons in that form, with occasional preachments in sporting ethics, an unbridled boyishness about the fun of outdoor adventure, and a teacher's awareness that instruction is usually best offered through relating the author's personal experience. Few since have achieved his quality of performance, but at least they knew who to imitate.

The magnitude of Roosevelt's influence on later writers is most immediately evident from the frequency with which they invoke his name. Nothing, apparently, gives a modern outdoor writer a greater feeling of security, a surer sense of being on the right track, than referring the reader to something "good ol' Teddy Roosevelt" once said. They speak familiarly of him, as if they are quoting not from his books but from a lunch conversation they had just last week. He is a symbol, never mind that no real friend of his would ever have called him "Teddy" to his face.

This is not to say that outdoor writing has not changed since Roosevelt's death. In the eight decades since then, fishing and hunting have changed more than in any previous three centuries, largely because of modified technology but also through the evolution of sporting ethics, that problematic bundle of perceptions and judgments that define what is good and what is not in sport. Outdoor writing reflects all those changes. But by Roosevelt's time, especially by the time of his death, the American outdoor writer was a mature type, and the forms of the writing were pretty much as they stand today.

There are two widely recognized types of outdoor writing. They have been given many labels, but perhaps the best were those offered by author-diplomat-cleric Henry Van Dyke. In *Fisherman's Luck* (1899), he called them "the literature of knowledge and the literature of power." The first is instructional, what the magazine editors call "how-to," and the second is meditative, sometimes inspirational, and usually experiential. The second, with its greater opportunity for rhetorical flight, is regarded as the higher form. Only a few writers can combine the two in one work, as Roosevelt did in his hunting books, or as A. J. McClane did more recently in *The Practical Fly Fisherman* (1953). The greater rhetorical opportunity leads naturally to greater literary risk, and however dismayed William Humphrey may have been by the fishing manuals, their offenses rarely match those of "fine" outdoor writing.

But the two types have not found equal application to all outdoor subjects. Some pursuits generate more of one than of the other. Deer hunting, for instance, has acquired a blue-collar image; it seems, for some reason that I can't understand, to lack poetic possibilities. For every ten instructional manuals on how to get your deer, there may be one book that celebrates the experience.

There are social issues here that, for the sake of outdoor writing's fraternal tone, are perhaps best left unexplored, but by contrast, upland bird shooters seem to produce a more even balance, perhaps even writing more celebrations than instructions. Deer hunting is to upland bird hunting as bait fishing is to fly-fishing; bait fishing accounts primarily for manuals, while fly-fishing is perhaps richest of all the blood sports in its exotic celebrations of itself.

Fly-fishing does generate a huge volume of technical writing, magnificently impenetrable books on entomological issues. I own many of these books; there is great comfort in possessing such vast, tidy, and enthusiastically unified information, even if I rarely use it. But fly-fishing also has raised the spiritual celebration of sport to new levels with books that threaten to remove themselves entirely from the act of catching a fish, replacing that apparent vulgarity with extensive philosophical dialogue and travel writing. I own even more of these books, and I even read them. Some I have read several times. I don't mind admitting that, though I know that many of them are not as well written as their authors may think, I still enjoy the stories immensely.

More difficult for me to deal with is the often clear message that these books send; they celebrate their sport, and themselves, with an unseemly confidence. Fly-fishing, more than the other sports, compels many of its writers to consider themselves superior, so that, for example, the late John Voelker (the "Robert Traver" who wrote *Anatomy of a Murder, People Versus Kirk*, and three very popular fishing books that I have often enjoyed) could proudly write that fly-fishing is to bait fishing as seduction is to rape.

Perhaps the last step in the scale of outdoor writing is big-game hunting. If you leave out the lowly deer and consider the more exotic game—bear, lion, elephant—you reach the opposite extreme from the dreary flood of books with names like *The Practical Deer Hunter*. For the big-game hunter, instructive writing is far less important than good yarns, probably because big-game hunters often have a guide to serve as instruction book. For every book on how to hunt lion, or bear, there are many on the joys of the experience. Thus do the various sporting writers reveal their literary prejudices and the instincts of their publishers.

But they all, from redneck deer hunter to Houston oil big-game hunter, are far more similar than they might realize. There are common threads in almost all the books, and the most evident is self-consciousness. For the modern outdoor book is almost as much a pulpit as it was in the hands of Theodore Roosevelt and, some would say, for good reason. The writers share an alarm over the world's perception of what they are doing, an alarm I think is justified. Readers, especially those of hunting books (fishing still hasn't attracted much attention from the mainstream anti–blood sport crowd in this country, but judging from what's going on in Europe, our turn will come), encounter the obligatory lectures on conservation and sportsmanship, lectures that, so many years after Forester and Roosevelt led the formalization of them, are growing more defensive. They seem less aimed at fellow sportsmen than at the general public, as if to say, "See, we do have standards and don't fit the stereotypes of killers and slobs." There is a need for self-justification here, one not found nearly as often in other specialty literatures such as bird watching or gardening. As important as some kind of defense may be, I doubt that these lectures are helping much.

So it is that in modern times, with less public understanding of pastimes that involve killing and eating wild creatures, outdoor writing struggles bravely with the forces that brought it here. One reads less gore-and-heroism (fewer slavering bears and lions) than one used to. I kind of miss them, but I'm frequently reminded by the advertisements in magazines, the pro-gun editorials, and an occasional hairy-chested adventure tale that the old Rooseveltian outdoor writer is not far below the surface. There are fewer of the old "me and Joe went fishin' " stories, those having been the backbone of that genre for decades, but the form has not died. It has been transmuted into what *Fishing World* editor Keith Gardner has called the "me and André went fishin' " story, an identical event in which people stay at costly lodges and talk about rare wines at streamside. A veneer of sophistication has been applied here and there, especially in stories about fly-fishing, whose already aristocratic pretensions may have reached a peak in 1970, when Arnold Gingrich descended from the World of Literature to become the sport's foremost commentator.

Those of us who care deeply about these sports, and who think their writing matters, watch the evolution of both with trepidation and hope. About the time I became involved in outdoor writing, in the 1970s, I was relieved to notice a maturing in content here and there. Some writers even mentioned sex in some context other than the spawning of trout or the rut of elk. In these new stories, people drank, lied, and cheated on their wives, all on the edge of outdoor experiences. Outdoor life, these new writers suggested, had something to do with real life, both the good and the bad.

I welcomed this development, but I don't expect too much of it. I recently sold a story to an outdoor magazine, a story with a fictional anecdote in it that concluded with a grizzly bear sticking a pistol up a hunter's ass. The editors changed "ass" to a more maidenly, and more anatomically improbable, "nose." Here, in magazines that were for much of their history largely supported by liquor and tobacco advertisements and that traditionally used pictures of nearly naked women to sell everything from outboard motors to sleeping bags, the readers were still encouraged to think that their fellow outdoorsmen talk like Natty Bumppo.

I date my own awareness of outdoor writing's broadening scope to Russell Chatham's hilarious story "The Great Duck Misunderstanding," published in *Gray's Sporting Journal* about twenty years ago (he later rewrote it for his book *Dark Waters*, but I like the original better). In this story, the author relates his conflicting urges when, after he's spent several days preparing for a duck dinner feast with friends, a gorgeous woman emerges unexpectedly from his past and invites him to spend that very evening with her. Caught between two powerful appetites, he succumbs to the ducks, but after the dinner, he unsuccessfully attempts to drag his bloated, flatulent self over to her place. This story, vivid and explicit, brought a response from offended matronly readers that I thought only further proved its worth.

Since then a countercultural school of outdoor writing has grown up, a kind of gonzo fly-fishing writing in which references to sex and other urges are almost obligatory and have therefore taken on an unconvincing tone. Where once outdoor writers felt a need to espouse fraternalism and good sport, some now feel equally required to offer asides about the gratification of other appetites. Like all fashions, sometimes it works, sometimes it doesn't.

But just as it's easy to praise outdoor writing on the basis of a relatively few really good writers, it's too easy to criticize it on the basis of stereotypically bad writing. These days, I see a lot less really bad writing in the outdoor magazines than was common twenty or thirty years ago. It appears to me that the average outdoor writer is better educated, less likely to make the kind of sophomoric grammatical errors that surprised Humphrey so much, and a lot savvier about the world beyond his duck blind than his predecessors (as are the editors who work with him). A few of the outdoor writers are even women, though I don't think that change is statistically significant yet.

For all its struggles with itself, I admire what outdoor writing is doing. For all its innocent delusions about its literary stature and its slightly less innocent delusions about what outdoor readers should read, it is holding onto something dear. I approve of hunting and fishing (and will even resist qualifying that statement to prove I'm a conservationist or love animals or am in general an admirable human being), and I like to read about them. I have read this stuff by the bale and written it by the ream. As good ol' Teddy Roosevelt said of hunting books, "Most of them are bad, of course, just as most novels and most poems are bad, but some of them are very good indeed . . ." Some recent or modern outdoor writers, in fly-fishing, for example—Roderick Haig-Brown, Russell Chatham, Charles Waterman, Steve Raymond, Ted Leeson, Harry Middleton, John Gierach, Christopher Camuto, and Nick Lyons come to mind right off—can hold their own as stylists with essayists in most other fields. (I find my own bias emerging here; some of these writers are so good I stumble when I try to call them outdoor writers.)

But T.R. was right: The best outdoor writing is not representative, any more than the best novels are representative of what you find on the drugstore racks. The best outdoor writing is not the mainstream, and it is not most of what I read. I know many literate people who happily suspend taste to read fishing and hunting stories written by people who, no matter how poorly they write, fish and hunt very well indeed. I know just as many who happily desert some "real world" for the reassuring anachronisms of outdoor writing because they, like Ed Zern, the late dean of outdoor humorists, "get all the truth I need in the newspaper every morning" and want something else from their recreational reading.

If outdoor writing seems tasteless to the outsider it is because it appeals to a different kind of taste. It is a sort of camp talk in print, the talk that Faulkner once called "forever the best of all listening." It is the talk of remembrance and the talk of hope. Novelist John Buchan once called fishing "a perpetual series of occasions for hope." The hook and bullet press multiplies those occasions, and readers ought to be a little forgiving if the hopes are not quite as well expressed as they might be.

I would have let this essay go at that, but when my editor, Bob Bender, read the manuscript of this book, he wrote the following note in the margin:

> I thought you were going to say that just as most fishing is hope unfulfilled, so most hook and bullet reading is unsatisfying—leaving us to appreciate the instances that are satisfying.

Well, yes, I would have said that, if only I'd thought of it.

Twelve

TROUT
FAMILY VALUES

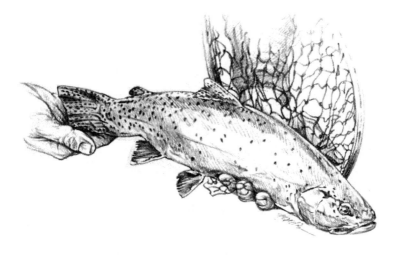

M Y HOME in Yellowstone is in good part surrounded by a network of small, undistinguished streams that, because of the park's many famous, big-trout waters, will probably stay relatively anonymous among guidebook writers. After all, when the Madison, or the Yellowstone, or the Firehole might yield a really big trout, and have such great name-dropping cachet besides, why fish some unknown creek 3 feet across for 5-inch brookies?

That's what I say too. Then I go and fish them. They're close to home, they're as beautiful as trout streams get anywhere, and I have to admit, I kind of like 5-inch brookies. They're fast, they're forthright in their opinions, and there is no more beautiful animal on earth.

These aren't secret streams, though (there probably isn't such a thing in Yellowstone, and if there were you wouldn't hear about it from me). They're right along roads, and they get fished hard by daily hordes of casual tourists and the occasional brookie enthusiast.

I, like the well-known first grader, don't always play nicely with others, so I tend to drift farther from the road than most people. Once the road and the other people are out of sight, it's just me and the trout. Oh, and a few elk herds, stunning mountains in the distance, the smell of the sage, the occasional call of a meadowlark or a sandhill crane, and everything else that makes Yellowstone's landscape so absorbing, distracting, and gloriously wild. At a time and place like that, a 5-inch trout is about as good a fish as I could stand.

In 1944, the prominent fisheries biologist Albert S. Hazzard, one of the pioneers of catch-and-release fishing, wrote an article in *Outdoor America* about trout fishing in national parks. He complained, correctly, that the National Park Service was catering to the "uneducated desires of the mob" by stocking catchable-size fish rather than relying on natural reproduction and scientifically based regulations to maintain robust wild trout populations in the supposed wilderness-quality waters of the parks.

Hazzard was something of a prophet of what the parks would eventually attempt to accomplish with fisheries management. Again and again, the parks, because of their unusual legislative mandates to preserve native species in a wild setting, would serve as important testing grounds for progressive management of fish and fishermen. They have given us many lessons, based on both success and failure, lessons with applications far beyond their boundaries.

But in another sense, Hazzard's vision may have been less clear. In discussing park lakes that could not sustain natural reproduction, he proposed that good fishing should be provided by introducing eyed eggs or fingerlings that would grow into "fine, highly colored, fighting trout—wild in every respect."

Since then, national park management philosophy has evolved to the point where many originally fishless lakes are not stocked at all. Under the Park Service's policies and legislative mandates, a large, nonnative predator like a trout introduced into a small alpine lake is only wild in the sense of being wildly inappropriate. To an ecologist, the lake is not, in the fisherman's language, "barren." It is full of life, a unique and precious little ecosystem that has spent thousands of years developing its community of native species of invertebrates, reptiles, amphibians, and plants. Among a park's many constituencies are a lot of people for whom a whole native ecosystem like that is worth much more than yet another fishing hole.

But park goals aside for a moment, I'm interested in Dr. Hazzard's definition of wild trout. To him, a trout that grew up in the water, even if it was planted there as a fingerling, was wild. That view was easily justified, at least for his purposes, because the fish had to become a functioning part of its new home in order to survive and grow; it had to find food and shelter and evade predators, thus becoming thoroughly adapted to the place. In Hazzard's view, any fish that achieved all that deserved to be called wild. On the other hand, fish that were just dumped out of a truck tank into the water last week as adults and were still swimming around in confusion when they were hooked, did not.

I can still recall the amusement in the voice of a fisheries biologist friend of mine who, upon returning from a "wild trout" conference in the early 1980s, reported that everybody there had a different definition of "wild." Today, relatively few fishermen and even fewer managers would call a stocked fingerling wild, even if it spent several years in the water before being caught. Our standards and values have changed and our understanding of wild ecosystems has evolved so that we have higher expectations when we insist on wild trout in our streams. We just don't agree on those expectations. Moreover, we are still a little unsure about how wild we really want our trout to be.

Much of this change in attitude is a logical outgrowth of rising environmental awareness. In the 1940s, only a few people, like Dr. Hazzard, were concerned with the philosophical implications of altered natural settings. Now those implications are a central topic in many wildlife management circles.

There are also more formal definitions of wild trout. Among managers, these definitions still pertain to how much time the fish has spent in the stream, but now that time is measured in generations rather than in the lifetime of one fish. A fish stocked as an egg or a fry isn't likely to be called wild; a fish whose grandparents were stocked in the stream is.

But wild isn't the same as native, and among managers, conservationists, and a growing number of fishermen, native is getting to be the important word. As we have introduced non-native fish not only to fishless waters but also to waters containing native fish, we have lowered a kind of ecological eggbeater into some glorious native ecosystems, resulting in changes that, though they may have been wonderful for fishermen, were disastrous for these beautiful little worlds that had been cranking along just fine without our help since the last ice age. Now that concepts like biodiversity and the conservation of native ecosystems are becoming a big deal, there is another way to measure wildness, one that applies directly to fishing.

Most fishermen may still adhere to the old view that "just so there's lots of fish for me to catch, I don't care what species they are," but at the management conferences and in conservationist circles there's much more talk about the importance of catching fish in their native settings. Look around any trout state and you're likely to see a few underfunded biologists working on identifying relict populations and "heritage" strains of native fish and talking about the importance of preserving some of the unique habitats that were homes to such fish. We now read of fishermen who keep "life lists" of fish they've caught, much as bird-watchers keep lists of species they've sighted, and who make pilgrimages to distant trout waters not merely because they've heard there are lots of fish to catch but because they want to participate in that particular setting and catch the fish that were shaped by that habitat.

In short, since Hazzard's time, wild-trout fishing has become more and more a setting-dependent sport. For centuries, fishing writers have stressed the importance of the surroundings—of fishing in beautiful places, whether their definition of beautiful required a manicured rural countryside or a howling wilderness. Even in George Gibson's time, 170 years ago, the beauty of the Letort and its sister streams was in good part the beauty of the grand old farmhouses, barns, fences, and other human structures that ordered and ornamented the neighboring farmlands.

Now, the fish and the setting are becoming more integral; the best setting, according to this new view, is the setting that still has the trout that developed there in the first place, whether they have survived continually or we have restored them. But we still have some hard questions to answer and some hard decisions to make. Letting trout be totally wild, and enjoying them on the terms that "totally wild" implies, isn't as simple as it sounds.

It is a common human vanity to assume that the earth as we see it today is somehow a finished product. Landscape ecologists—most ecologists, for that matter—know better, and the ones with a sense of humor get a kick out of our attitudes. All the processes that shaped the modern American landscape, whether geological, biological, or climatic, are still acting today, unless we change them or stop them, which we often do for good reasons. Nature isn't done with our trout streams.

We tend to see trout as finished products too, as if around 1800 or so, evolution dropped them off at our door and said, "Have a nice time." But if we're really serious about wild trout, we must admit that it's not like that. Trout, like the rivers and lakes they inhabit, exist in a state of change. Sometimes the change is subtle, sometimes it is spectacular, but however it occurs it is the rule without exception in the wild. When we make trout and trout streams into something we find more suitable to our own tastes, we may be producing wonderful fishing, but we are not taking wild-trout fishing to its logical conclusion. We are, of course, in charge, and so we get to do whatever we like with our trout and our streams, but we could stand to think about it all a little more.

We fishermen don't like big disturbances in our trout streams. We hate hundred-year floods, when we find our trout in the trees. We are even annoyed by less catastrophic spring runoff when it lasts longer than suits our schedule and keeps us from fishing. We worry that anchor ice, extreme low or warm water, and a hundred other threats will reduce our trout populations, which is to say we don't want any of these things to interefere with our catch rate. In fact, we tend to view all of these largely natural processes with the same disapproval that we view human-caused problems, such as pollution or agricultural dewatering of trout streams. But here's the question we need to ask ourselves more often: How much dare we compromise the native ecosystem's integrity without ruining the wildness of our trout fishing?

The poet Robinson Jeffers asked: "What but the wolf's tooth whittled so fine / The fleet limbs of the antelope?" Far less poetically but at least bluntly, I would ask: What but the wild river's unbridled power shaped / Every single quality we love in trout? The very forces that had so much to do with creating the trout we admire—the violent extremes of environment that provided these species with the tests that turned them into our favorite fish—are a critical part of their wildness.

I admit we've come a long way. Only a couple of generations ago, leading fishing authorities forcefully recommended the indiscriminate shooting of herons, otters, mergansers, mink, and any other wild animal that competed with us for trout, just as leading hunting authorities gleefully blasted every wolf they saw. We don't hear much about that kind of foolishness anymore. We're even being kinder to the so-called forage fish, begrudgingly admitting that they have a role to play in a wild trout stream even if we aren't yet acknowledging that they have a place just because they're a legitimate native species.

I also admit that in many places, for social, political, and ecological reasons, we have created trout fisheries that can never be "wild" in any grand sense. Public recreational needs demand such fisheries, and they are often very good. I'm not preaching revolution against all other kinds of trout fishing here; not quite, at least. I'm just trying to clarify where we are in our search for wild trout.

As seems to happen often in fisheries management, Yellowstone National Park provides some engaging examples of the dilemmas of wild-trout management, examples that I hope will reach far beyond the boundaries of the park. The fires of 1988, so ill-reported in the media, swept across hundreds of thousands of acres and many watersheds, jarring the entire ecological system along the way. In a couple of small, narrow drainages where the heat was most intense, there were some pretty big fish kills, but for the most part the short-term effects of the fire on the fish were minimal. But the long-term effects are something else.

Fortunately, in recent years a great deal of ecological research had been done on Yellowstone's vegetation and the role fire played here back before the park was established in 1872. Tree-ring studies showed that fire worked on this landscape episodically, rather than annually. Most years, lightning strikes might ignite a few small fires. In much drier years, those strikes might burn several thousand acres. And once in awhile, a long while, when the right combination of fuel and climatic conditions prevailed, some threshold of volatility would be crossed and huge chunks of forest and meadow would burn. The fire return interval for the park's extensive lodgepole pine forests was 250 to 400 years; it took about that long for the extreme fuel loads of a very old forest to accumulate, and once it did all you needed was a really dry year. In 1988, it got so dry that even marsh vegetation burned, and a series of six powerful cold fronts brought high winds that drove the flames on and on, into the headlines and onto the television news, where they were often misunderstood. In Yellowstone, a cycle that had occurred dozens of times before started again. As soon as it was over, nature did the next thing, which was to start the whole process over and grow new trees.

Most of the fire-management specialists, ecologists, and others who seriously studied the fires, including a couple of famous "blue-ribbon" panels of experts, agreed that, yes, this is how Yellowstone works. Some of them even celebrated the beauty of all this natural freedom. After all, it was just what happens when things are allowed to be wild.

But as some fishermen who visited the park in 1989 noticed, up close it's a little more complicated than that. They found some of their favorite trout pools surrounded by blackened forests, places that, though already covered with the first new green growth, would lack the old photogeneity for many years, probably longer than the fishermen's remaining lifetimes.

For these people, picturesqueness and stability were more important than naturalness, and I do have some sympathy for them. If you only had a few days to spend here, and that week a summer thunderstorm washed a huge amount of loose ash down through your favorite stream, the fires of 1988 would seem like a pretty awful thing. Trout fishing, these people felt, shouldn't be quite *this* wild.

But even if the thousands of firefighters who spent the summer here had been able to stop these fires, I'm convinced it would have been a bad idea. No one can claim to care more about Yellowstone fish and fishing than I do, or to feel more indebted to these wonderful streams for all they've added to my life, but here, at least, we can define wild trout as trout that live in a really wild place—not a perfect wildness, but a remarkably good imitation of a North American landscape prior to the arrival of Columbus.

As it turned out, the major park fisheries showed relatively little effect in terms of how the fishing held up. National Park Service managers, who are forced by law to stand back far enough from a situation like this to see its big effects as well as the annoyance to this or that individual visitor, were reassured by a whole batch of scientific studies, and also by the postfire surveys and studies conducted by the U.S. Fish & Wildlife Service. It turned out that the catch rate in park waters did not change. For a few years after 1988, the average size of fish caught actually increased a little, a possible response to a flush of nutrients released by the fires. In those first few years after the fires, fishermen averaged more fish caught, and the indices of angler satisfaction (something I don't believe any survey can fully measure, but I guess they have to try) with fish size and the fishing experience both reached new highs. In all, if one wanted to worry about threats to good fishing in Yellowstone, the fires had to rank well below overcrowding, bad manners, poaching, introduction of exotic species, and every other known problem the park faces.

But this is a national park, with a different definition of harm anyway. The park's goal is to preserve something bigger than this or that favorite species. By legal and policy definition, the park is there to preserve the community of life forms and the processes that maintain and shape that community. By these same definitions, the fires did *no* harm to the park; they were just an unusually energetic and exciting part of the processes. The same forces that brought us the fires of 1988 brought us wild trout. If we want authentic wild trout in an authentic wild setting, the fires are part of the price that must be paid.

I know how nervous this kind of talk makes people; it's dangerously close to "tree-huggin' 'nvarnmental ex*tree*mism." But we owe our wild trout to some pretty extreme environments, and if defending such places makes me a tree-hugger, fine.

Having the luxury of living in the park, I also have the luxury of being philosophical about the fires. But people who complained about streams that ran black with ash during thunderstorms in 1989 should remember that those thunderstorms would have happened whether the fires of 1988 happened or not; the high, roiled water would still have been high, roiled water, just as unfishable whatever its color. This is a young, raw landscape, and its fishing is vulnerable to a host of such sudden disappointments.

On July 30, 1997, I tried to fish my local stream here in the park, and found it still high, murky, and in some places out of its banks due to last winter's extraordinary snowpack and a series of intense thunderstorms that summer. Now that my memory of this stream reaches back twenty-five years, I can confidently say that if all I cared about in Yellowstone was fishing, I would happily trade the fishing opportunities of 1989, weird as the water may have looked with all that ash, for either of the past two years, when this landscape experienced a stunning amount of precipitation. But fishing is only one of the things I care about here, so I just began my fishing season later than usual and was pleased to think that the additional water meant that the fishing would stay lively through the dog days of late summer. Wild-trout waters make us no guarantees, and I like it that way.

Our sense of scale as fishermen is pretty short. We become impatient with nature, which has no sympathy for our short lives. Therefore we do many things to wild-trout ecosystems. We often have to do them just to restore the fishing, but we sometimes go well beyond what nature would do if nature were in charge again. We take a trout stream and reshape it to our purposes with bulldozers and diversions and all sorts of architectural intrusions, usually to increase its productivity of trout. Often, nature comes back through and "corrects" our changes, blowing out our little dams and rolled rocks and other habitat alterations. So we do them again, because we know what we want from our trout fishing.

We likewise do many things to wild trout. We are getting better and better at engineering trout to suit any environment; some courageous souls have even tried to selectively harvest their local trout to release and thereby favor fish that rise to dry flies. Countless times we have introduced nonnative trout to a new stream or lake. Then we have either ignored their effects on the native fish, or actively sought to remove those natives, perhaps even introducing nonnative forage fish to further complicate the evolutionary crapshoot we've set in motion. We do all these things, and in no time at all we're celebrating the high quality of the "wild-trout fishing" we find there.

I have benefited beyond measure from these things we do to trout streams and trout. From the highest and smallest Sierra creek to the lowland rivers that empty onto the eastern Piedmont, I've immersed myself in the joy of this great pursuit and the wonder of the fish I am always surprised to catch. But I'm enough of a naturalist to know that there's something different—something tangible and important—about the brook trout I catch in the Sierra creek and the superficially identical fish I catch in the Virginia Blue Ridge. Neither fish is less a marvel, but in evolutionary terms, one has the weight of thousands of years behind its occupancy of its little pool, and the other arrived just shortly before I did. Context makes the catching different in a way that matters to me even if it doesn't lessen my delight.

Distinctions of this sort still don't have a lot of effect on most trout-management decisions, but we need to be thinking about how we see our wild trout. We must because they and their aquatic worlds matter to more and more people all the time. National parks aren't the only places where nonfishermen are taking an interest in fish—where the fish *watchers* outnumber the fishermen. The entire world is now the sphere of conservation biologists and other people who view nature as a whole and as a process. The previous generations of fisheries managers and fishermen are now seen as the chief culprits in the diminution or destruction of thousands of native aquatic systems, and the remaining waters that are still in pretty good shape are guarded jealously. The most stupid and selfish fishermen among us do great harm to our public image by clandestinely introducing some favorite exotic fish into some defenseless lake or stream, setting off another set of ecological ripples that will further reduce the true wildness of yet another native place. Throughout the American West, this kind of "Johnny Appleseed mentality" has reached epidemic proportions.

We fishermen need to be on better behavior, not only because we are no longer the only people who care about these waters, but also because fishing is bound to get increasing attention from the same people who are currently making life so hard for hunters—people who just can't imagine what fun it could be to kill or, even worse, hook, terrify, and then release such beautiful, wild creatures as trout. The extent to which we can fight off those attacks will be the extent to which we show sympathy for the needs of wild-trout ecosystems and thereby show that we are still the best friends wild trout have.

Which brings me back to those little brook trout streams near my home. Many of them were barren of fish life when the park was created; the brookies (and in at least one place, a few rainbows) that were stocked in them more than a century ago replaced no native fish, though they may have had some effects on the rest of the streams' fauna. Now, after all these years, these nonnative fish are becoming something special not only as beautiful animals but as scientific baselines.

In several places in Yellowstone, fish stocked back in the park's early days were the only stockings made. They were unloaded, sent on their way, and never tinkered with again. Without meaning to, early managers were setting up little gene banks of trout strains, isolated and kept free from the swirl of genetic confusion that was visited upon so many native fish by intensive hatchery operations in North America since those days. That means that now Yellowstone's nonnative fish may in some few cases be the purest examples of what those fish were once like.

The most notorious instance of this may be the lake trout, which was not native to Yellowstone Park but was introduced to a few larger waters around the turn of the last century. On the one hand, the descendants of the lake trout placed in Lewis Lake back then have recently been used as brood stock in efforts to restore that species to the Great Lakes. Ironically, Yellowstone's lake trout populations, unmanipulated and left alone for a century, became valuable to their home waters, and their presence in the park, even though they were nonnative, took on a new meaning.

On the other hand, within the past twenty years or so, some moron illegally introduced lake trout into Yellowstone Lake, the last great stronghold of the Yellowstone cutthroat trout. The cutthroats have spent ten thousand years adapting to a lake with no larger fish predator, and much of their chosen behavior makes them easy prey for the much larger lake trout, which now threaten to annihilate them. For every single time we've gotten lucky and accidentally done something that would help our descendants (like save a healthy lake trout population in Lewis Lake), there are hundreds of times that we have destroyed something priceless in the name of good fishing.

I don't usually give a lot of thought to all this as I sneak up on the next deep spot on my little brook trout rivers. But every once in a while, when I pause to admire one of these fish, I get a flash of memories of the Blue Ridge, the Green Mountains, the Smokies, or some other place where I've similarly admired its kin. Then my mind is off on another rumination of how far these trout traveled on their own, and how much farther they came with our help, and I can't help feeling that we'd have been better off to leave them alone.

Thirteen

NOW I ARE ONE

I N 1997, I enjoyed the great and almost unimaginable honor of being awarded an honorary doctorate of letters by Montana State University. There at Bozeman, under the watchful eyes of some eleven thousand people, M.S.U. President Mike Malone (a fellow historian, I took great comfort to realize) read a glowing statement about me, two deans lowered the hood over my shoulders, and I hurried back to my chair on the podium, clutching my diploma with enough shaky pride to leave fingerprints.

Later that morning, I was invited to return to the podium for the commencement ceremony of "my" school, arts and letters. At the beginning of that ceremony, attended by a few thousand, the dean in charge introduced several honored guests on the podium. When she came to me, she described me as "Paul Schullery, author and fly fisherman." Afterwards, at a wonderful luncheon at Mike's house, Bud Lilly, longtime Montana outfitter and friend, and I shook our heads in wonderment that the day had come when just being a fly fisherman would be a distinction worth noting on such an occasion.

When I started fly fishing in the early 1970s, I read all of the worshipful portrayals of the "greats and near-greats" of fly-fishing who became minor celebrities in those days. Like many other fly fishermen, I was swept along on the wave of excitement that the sport experienced then, when it seemed that every few months another new and even more skillful master emerged on the lecture tour. Book sales must have been fabulous.

But eventually I got cynical. I wondered if these guys could really be as good as their reputations. Standing along some stream, strangling in my latest errant back cast, I found it hard to believe it wasn't like this for everyone.

As I have already explained, my years in charge of a fly-fishing museum brought me close to the heart of this sport and gave me the opportunity to get to know some of the best fishermen around. I have since been able to fish with a lot of experts, some famous, some infamous, some pretty much unknown but no less impressive. Now, after many years exploring this lofty world, I bring back word of what these people are like.

First, I must offer assurances to my fellow leader stranglers that there really are people who catch fish almost on command. Some of them are even better than you've heard. Some of them aren't as good as they seem to think, but some of them are amazing.

Some were true vagabonds, like the energized Parisian who

zoomed into Vermont when I lived there and attacked the Battenkill with a furious enthusiasm previously spent on waters in Africa, Europe, Canada, and even Asia. "It's fabulous in Katmandu," he told me, "very cheap hashish and the finest trout fishing."

Some were less satisfying examples of what fishing does to people, self-proclaimed experts and skeptics like the visiting spin fisherman I encountered as I was walking back to my car after an evening's fishing on the Battenkill near Arlington. I knew instantly that it was a mistake to talk to him; he had the aggressive bearing of a person who, if we had been children, I would have avoided on the playground at all costs. But there was no escaping him; as I sat on my tailgate and wrestled out of my vest and waders, he droned on and on, that the river was "overrated, yes, highly overrated. I only caught fourteen fish." He was belligerently smug, and I think he expected me to be impressed he'd caught so many—fourteen fish is an outstanding evening on the Battenkill—when in fact I was only made curious, for the hundredth time in my wanderings of American rivers, about why a sport as nice as fishing should attract such self-important jerks.

Some of the jerks were supposed experts, the famous ones who, in their books at least, seemed able to catch fish anywhere, and they may have been the most revealing of all. For it is a matter of considerable local amusement that, for all the Battenkill's renown as a great trout river, some of these famous masters (Robert Traver calls them "the Learned Society of Elder Swamis") rarely seemed to get around to writing about their fishing here, or if they did, they were mysteriously quiet about what they actually caught. The Battenkill at its hardest is as hard as it gets.

But many experts were the real thing. One evening, John

Merwin, who worked for *Fly Fisherman* before establishing *Fly Rod & Reel*, took me and a visiting friend of mine out in his canoe on a small mountain lake near Manchester. This was about the time that John's book on lake fly-fishing was published, and he was getting a lot of good press as a cool hand.

My friend Bill was a serious outdoorsman from the Midwest, but despite my attempts to interest him in fly-fishing a few years earlier, he had still done very little of it. He clamped himself firmly in the middle of the canoe and refused to fish at all in the presence of such veterans. John rowed us around for an hour or so, long enough for me to catch one or two small fish and start to feel like maybe I even deserved to fish with the big kids. Bill was impressed.

Then John rowed to a shallow weed bed at one end of the lake, picked up his rod, and made his first cast. He had a nondescript little nymph on, the sort of fly that if I saw it on my own line I'd just assume was a scraggly, late-night mistake at the fly-tying vise, but that, seen there on a real fishing-book author's line, had a nearly mystical quality for me: The vague scruffiness became scientific purposefulness, an obviously inspired example of imitative impressionism, combining an indistinct outline with muted yet distinct shadings that would catch the murky subaquatic light just so. . . . Of such is the kingdom of fly-fishing authority.

On that first cast, John took a 16-inch brown, a beautiful, heavy lake fish that dazzled my friend and, I must admit, me. For my audience, however, I took a grumpier view and pretended to treat it more lightheartedly. "You know," I told John as he was releasing the fish, "if you were smart you wouldn't cast again." We all laughed at the implication that the catch was just dumb luck, but my friend and I knew where we stood: in an expert's presence.

My most illuminating exposures to expertise in Vermont

were my many fishing trips with John Harder, then in charge of Orvis's huge retail fly operation. He caught difficult fish with such ease, while talking, smoking, laughing, and otherwise acting like a regular mortal, that I began to imagine that it was possible for me to get really *good* at this. I was wrong, of course. I lacked the combination of temperament, hand-eye coordination, and intellectual discipline to do what he did, though I think he made me a better fisherman just through the inspiration of his example.

I saw John do what experts do in their own self-promotion: catch truly uncatchable fish. The most impressive of all was a riser on the Battenkill at Manchester, where the stream oozed slick and slow through a tunnel of overhanging tree limbs. What with the low, leafy roof, it was a caster's nightmare, and the current was so slight and smooth that even careful wading sent waves a hundred feet *up*stream, putting down all risers even before I could get close enough to scare the devil out of them with my cast.

As we stood at the downstream end of this tunnel one still, sultry day, we spotted a good fish way up in the shadiest part, rising steadily under the protection of the brush along one bank. Alone, I would have ignored it, or just tossed an insult its way as I moved on. But John went after it.

I watched him do the impossible, and I still don't know how he did it. He didn't use any incantations or potions. He made it look like it was just something people did. He waded to within casting range (this was clearly impossible), scoped out the fish's vulnerability (it had none), put a fly over it (it was sure to race off in a panic, but didn't), raised it, hooked it, and brought it to net. It was a 16-inch brookie, a grand trout for that water. It seemed almost unfair, sometimes, that John was allowed to use both hands.

Making the difficult look easy seems to be a trait of experts. A few years after I'd moved from Vermont back to Montana, I spent a summer fishing southeastern Montana with Bud Lilly, more or less the dean of Western fly-fishing guides (we told our wives it was "field research" for the books we were writing). One day we stood side by side in the Yellowstone River, casting identical flies over one group of rising trout, and he outfished me six to one. My casts may not have been as good as his, but come on—six to one?

Bud captured the essence of expertise on another occasion, and luckily the lesson was shared beyond me. Partway through the year that Bud and I fished together, my wife Dianne and I realized it was time to leave Montana and get real jobs. In four years I'd reached the point where I was making a passable living at writing, but I was burned out on it, and Dianne's career as an editor was showing real promise that couldn't be fulfilled in Livingston. We also thought the move might be good for a failing marriage, and we discovered we both liked the idea of trying to live in Hershey, Pennsylvania, for a while. Though leaving the Yellowstone country always saddened me beyond words, I knew we had to do this.

So we asked Bud's wife, Esther, who was both a friend and a realtor, to list our house for us. This happened just after the big railroad shop in Livingston closed. House prices dropped hugely, so selling the house even at a big loss seemed unlikely, what with all the railroad people leaving town and selling theirs.

But Esther was unintimidated and announced we were going to have an open house. She put an ad in the *Enterprise* and gave Dianne her orders: make a big pot of coffee and a lot of chocolate-chip cookies. This was as much for what the aroma added to the mood and atmosphere of the house as for anything that the visitors might want to eat. She explained that people walk into a place that looks nice and smells like mother's kitchen and they're halfway sold. Dianne and I were really nervous about all this, so right before the open house was to start, Bud took us fishing and left Esther, the cookies, and the house, to their fate.

Bud took us 60 miles, up to the park, to one of the little rivers I'd fished often in the 1970s when I lived there. It was the middle of a bright, hot day, and the fishing was very slow. Dianne, a competent fly fisher with much better vision than mine, spotted a fish rising against a tangle of snags and worked a dry fly over it for about ten minutes without success before I came along. She invited me to try the fish, and I did no better. Then Bud came by, so we invited him to take a turn.

For all the satisfactions in a day's fishing, I seem to fish especially for those singular little illuminations that make the sport so engaging: a heron rising from a gravel bar, a fish flashing deep for a nymph, or a hilarious offhand remark by a companion. The window opens, the light comes in, the day is made, and somehow I'm a little changed. As Bud waded in at the tail of the pool, the opening of the window was almost audible.

I said something quietly to Dianne about watching closely, but it was unnecessary; she knew. For ten minutes, with no self-conscious intention or spoken instruction, Bud gave her a lesson in how to fish a trout pool.

It was of no consequence that he did catch a fish. What mattered was the series of perfectly placed casts—here a reach cast, there a little slack for a longer drift up against the snag—that showed the searching fly at its best. What mattered was the example of principle, that there really was a right way, and beyond that a supremely right way, to do all this. What mattered wasn't whether or not she could absorb and copy every little trick he had, or every intuition he revealed about where the trout might be holding. What mattered was the glimpse she got, through a gifted eye, out the open window.

The light that comes in at a time like that doesn't simply vanish; it lingers and brightens your fishing for a long time. And even when the moment has passed and routine is restored, the window never seems to close quite as tight again.

Oh, and Esther, an expert in her own right, found a buyer for the house that day.

When we got to Hershey, in southern Pennsylvania, Dianne became an editor at Stackpole Books, the venerable publisher of outdoor books, which meant that I was fortunate enough to meet Ed Koch, whom she persuaded to do a new edition of his midge-fishing book. Ed, in the best tradition of George Gibson, is one of the modern masters of the "limestoners," and getting to know him was a great treat. One day at his house he showed me the 9-pound trout he'd taken on a little Letort cricket back in the sixties, a fish I'd seen pictured and read about in Charlie Fox's *This Wonderful World of Trout*. The thing was so huge and untroutlike, it looked like a varnished wind sock.

One hot morning, Ed and I were fishing Clark Creek, north of Harrisburg; this was still, low, clear water, and the fish were holding a few inches beneath the surface but not rising much. Ed was fishing his little twine shrimp by wading literally right up behind the fish (again, why didn't they run away?), casting little more than the leader (that's how close he was), then watching the fish. The moment a fish's head turned slightly, Ed knew it was taking the invisible little fly, and he'd set the hook. It worked every time. "See, Paul? It's easy . . ."

That's another thing about experts, bless their hearts. They really do think it's easy.

I've been thrilled to get to fish with these guys and to learn a few things from them, but lately I've noticed a disturbing trend. People are starting to treat *me* like an expert. This is not a complete mystery; I think it's the result of "expertise by association." After all, I've been hanging out with these guys for years, I spent five years as director of a fly-fishing museum, and eventually wrote or cowrote several books about it. Ed Koch even persuaded me to write the foreword for the second edition of his book on midge fishing (and an especially windy foreword it turned out to be, all full of historical ruminations and stuff that could lead the reader to think I know something about actually catching fish). This sort of thing snowballs, so I've probably written forewords for eight or ten fishing books now.

Now, I know what you're probably thinking; you've looked at the jacket of this book and thought to yourself "Paul *who?*" My response exactly; I still don't think of myself as someone I should have heard of. I'm still making those same rotten casts I did twenty years ago. But this expert business isn't simple. Because of all this stuff I've been involved in, and because of all my writing, I've been noticed. It thrills me when my books get good reviews, because they're very important to me, but it does have this odd side effect. A number of people now think of me as a prominent fisherman, which they apparently assume means someone who can catch fish.

It took Dianne and me less than two years in Hershey to wrap up the last of our marriage and part friends, which meant that in 1988, when the fires of Yellowstone became national news, I was ready to come home. In August of that year, my friends in the park offered me a job writing about the fires, and I bailed out of a fairly uninteresting job in Harrisburg, packed, and raced across the country in time to see some pretty spectacular flames and immediately embroil myself in the park's endless controversies and wonders.

Not long after I returned, I was introduced to a large gathering (a couple hundred people, sitting there to hear me talk about fish natural history) as the man who knew more about Yellowstone fishing than anyone else. This was a compliment of staggering generosity, because I could look around the room and point to a few people who actually might *deserve* such an introduction. But one thing I'd already learned about the authority game is that a compliment like that is as durable as an ugly rumor. It's like a bullet: you can't call it back. I've tried. Any denial I offered would be waved aside as modesty, or greeted with annoyance as *false* modesty. There's no recovering from such a devastating compliment; it's better just to pretend it wasn't said. If those people could see me out on a stream, dragging wind knots the size of walnuts through the sage, most would just assume I was using some complex, arcane technique that only real experts understood. Only the real experts know better, and they're too polite to say anything.

This can only end badly. Eventually, someone who asks my advice on where to fish is going to arrive at the rancid mudhole I directed him to (protesting all the time, "I don't know much about it, but if you really want to go there, turn right at . . .") and realize it really *is* a rancid mudhole, not some secret spot he just doesn't have the skill to fish successfully. Then he'll also realize the problem is my advice, and that I must be one of those *phony experts!*

When *that* bullet leaves the gun, I've had it. People won't listen to me when I talk about the things I *do* have some expertise in. Trout Unlimited will revoke my patch. Envelopes to magazine editors will be returned unopened. The happy flow of free review copies of new books I get from publishers will dry up. Sales of my own books will drop from pitiful to pathetic.

But that rejection shouldn't be any worse than the kind I get from trout every day. And if it comes to that, I'll at least have the comfort of being back where I started, a perpetual beginner with an undiminished passion for what matters most in trout fishing. I never did expect any more.

I'll kind of miss the free books, though.

Fourteen

CUMBERLAND DREAMS

HILE the evening light was still strong, the little river seemed dead. We slipped into the warm water about 7:00. My companions, Rod Bond and Phil Hanyok, spread out upstream, Rod occasionally shouting vague commands at Captain Crunch, his huge black retriever. Crunch was an explorer and spent the whole evening churning up the shallow water and thrashing around in the streamside vegetation. Rod's periodic bellows did seem to have an effect in that they usually caused an immediate if random change in the dog's direction, but I don't think Crunch stopped rampaging around the whole night.

For the first hour or so, nothing happened. We saw no motion in the clear, shallow water, and I began to wonder if yet again I'd been brought to a great secret spot on the wrong night. Then, as the light was getting fairly weak, a few rises appeared here and there over the clean river bottom, in spots where we had seen no fish moments before. The risers were little sunfish and rock bass, eagerly wrestling good-sized mayflies through the surface film, and I welcomed them. As pretty as the Conodoguinet was, I was getting a little bored.

I had lived in Hershey, not far across the Susquehanna from all the most famous limestone spring creeks, when I was a child, and, later, passing through every few years, I always admired the gentle rolling country around Harrisburg. Years later, after I'd moved away, Vincent Marinaro's *A Modern Dry Fly Code*, with its loving descriptions and bucolic photographs of rural Pennsylvania, awakened in me an affection and nostalgia that grew from some of my sweetest childhood memories of life in a small town surrounded by flawless south Pennsylvania countryside. I soon put the area on my wish list of places I'd like to spend some time, a few years if possible.

I knew southern Pennsylvania was a fine country. I'd read about the trout fishing for years. The real surprise would be the diversity of the fishing. In 1986, John Randolph, then editor of both *Country Journal* and *Fly Fisherman*, hired me to work for him at the former. When, sitting in my front room in Livingston, Montana, he offered me the job, he tried to tell me how good the nontrout fishing was in Pennsylvania's Cumberland Valley. "I can leave the office and in a ten-minute drive be on the river catching bass." It was hard to believe, but now I do.

The river he was referring to was the Susquehanna, a giant bass stream with some of the heaviest mayfly hatches I've ever seen, emergences so thick that even large catfish abandon the river bottom and become steady risers. Two of my friends took

4-pound catfish on dries during the peak of the mayfly emergences, just at dark. At Fort Hunter, a few miles upstream from Harrisburg, the late-summer fly fisherman has miles of shallow fishing water with hardly any company, a kind of separation from other fishermen that I usually only associate with wilderness streams.

It was this improbable mix of waters that surprised me in 1986 when I returned to Pennsylvania, and that engaged the naturalist in me. Here, amidst a fabulous network of limestone trout streams, were perfect lowland rivers, heavy with sediment and warm enough to wade wet much of the season. I'd never seen such a variety of fishing in such a small space, and my only real regret when I left to return to Yellowstone in late 1988 was that I didn't begin to do the fishing justice in only two seasons. For me, nothing compares with Yellowstone, but I can still indulge in idle regrets, and the Conodoguinet has been the focus of some of my keenest regrets, at least as many as the Letort itself.

Conodoguinet Creek loops its way east across Cumberland County, receiving along the way the flow of any number of small spring creeks, including the Letort, and finally emptying into the Susquehanna at West Fairview, just across the river from Harrisburg. It is characterized, especially its last few miles as it winds through the suburban communities that line the west shore of the Susquehanna, by deeply entrenched meanders of textbook perfection. The river runs first north, then south, then north, then south, in reversal after reversal, a lethargic flat flow that seems more suitable to carp than smallmouth bass and often is.

On this particular evening Rod, Phil, and I were a few miles more upstream, where the development was still pretty thick but where some stretches of the riverbank weren't completely covered with house lots yet. I didn't drive that night, so I'm sure I couldn't find my way back. Getting there involved lots of turns down roads that either did not have signs, or had long before surrendered them to the sumac jungles that grow so freely along Cumberland roads.

As it grew dark, I could hear but not see Rod splashing and laughing as he hooked a good fish. Rod was then art director of *Fly Fisherman*. I occasionally escaped from my corner of the building, the *Country Journal* corner, where nobody talked fishing, to his, where everybody did, so I assumed that I would be regaled the next day with new claims of glory for his infamous "Flies from Hell" series. Rod had a jolly insufferability in success.

I had taken a few tiddlers on tiny streamers and dry flies, and my hopes of hooking one of the good smallmouths were just about gone. The side of the river opposite our car was the one with the most promise. Most of the water was open, 2 or 3 feet deep, and shelterless for larger fish, but the far shore showed some weed beds, where the current seemed to develop a few twists, and where bigger fish could hide.

I gradually had worked my way to within casting distance of such a place, and in the last bit of light I could make out some darker spots where water weeds came to the surface, indicating both depth and shelter downstream from them. I made a few tentative casts into the area with no effect and had essentially given up when I first heard the splashes of a big fish chasing something small. Dinnertime.

On a couple of trout streams over the years, I have had a little success at what is known in some circles as "sound fishing." It involves aiming the fly toward some noise you assume to be a fish. I'd had the foresight, back while I had any sight at all, to tie on a large deer-hair bass bug, and I now lofted it into the darkness.

It's difficult to explain how you know what you're doing at times like this. You've been casting for an hour or two, and through some combination of how long the line takes to turn over behind you, how heavy it feels as it does so, what you remember of how much line you were casting back when there was a little light, the occasional faint flash of a surface disturbance out there somewhere, and who knows what subliminal or even instinctive near-senses that kick in, you can actually put the fly pretty close to where you want it. I have a few memories of hearing trout rise when I could not see them at all and actually hooking them in only a few casts. Sometimes it all has a spooky dreamlike reason to it, like it's something at which you could become consistent.

It's spooky anyway. When your eyes can't help you, your other senses seem to go into overdrive; the river is suddenly noisy, breezes seem more aggressive, and your hackles rise a little in the dark. It pays to concentrate on the fish.

I did. I jerked the big bug back toward me with as much gurgling and splooshing as I could, and struck as soon as the next splash came. My leader was heavy, so I just stripped the line in fast, hauling the bass right to my feet. After a slippery moment, I got a good grip and lifted it up long enough to get a light on it and see it was a fat 14 or 15 inches. I unhooked it and pushed it on its way.

A few casts later, I did the same thing with its twin: hear the splash, take a sort of existential aim, and send the bug out to cover the sound. Set the hook in the next sound, and pull from it the fish. Haul it in, let it go, look around, and realize, with a surprise that I'm not entitled to after so many years and so many late nights fishing, that now I have to wade clear across the river in the dark.

It is one of fly-fishing's greatest deceptions, and greatest salvations, that after a long time when it seems impossible, it suddenly seems easy. It is probably the Conodoguinet's strongest attraction for me now, as I daydream my way through my fishing life, that on that last night I fished it, it saw me on my way so generously. And it is probably fly-fishing's best attraction for me that during all those times I can't be fishing, I can sustain my passion for it through just such dreams.

ACKNOWLEDGMENTS

I MUST first thank some friends I have made over the years, some of whom have shared the episodes described here, and all of whom have helped bring fishing's inherent magic to life for me: Larry Aiuppy, Jan Aiuppy, Bill Cass, Dale Greenley, John Harder, Richard Klukas, Ed Koch, Richard Kress, David Ledlie, Bud Lilly, John Merwin, Leon Martuch, Leigh Perkins, Perk Perkins, Randall Perkins, Dianne Russell, Steve Schullery, Mark Webster, and Craig Woods.

I must also thank a number of ecologists, some of whom I know as friends and some whom I've just been lucky enough to read, whose work and ideas have had a great influence on my own thinking about trout and their world: Robert Behnke, Don Despain, Robert Gresswell, Douglas Houston, Aldo Leopold, A. Starker Leopold, Paul Needham, and John Varley.

Then there are fishing's historical and philosophical writers (some of these are friends too), amateur and professional, popular and scholarly, from whose writings I have learned so much, even when I found it necessary to argue with their conclusions: John Betts, Conrad Voss Bark, Ken Cameron, Brian Curtis, Arnold Gingrich, Charles Goodspeed, Roderick L. Haig-Brown, Rachel Hands, Jack Heddon, John Waller Hills, Richard Hoffmann, Austin Hogan, David Ledlie, Ted Leeson, Nick Lyons, John McDonald, Ernest Schwiebert, Odell Shepard, and Charles Waterman.

Portions of this book appeared in very different form in the following publications: *The American Fly Fisher, Field & Stream, The Flyfisher, Fly Fishing Heritage, Gray's Sporting Journal, The New York Times, Pennsylvania Heritage, Rod & Reel,* and *Trout.* My thanks to those editors for their help and interest. An earlier version of chapter twelve was first presented as the keynote speech at the Wild Trout VI Conference in Bozeman, Montana, August 1997.

As in earlier books, I must thank Jean McCreight for typing various manuscripts and articles onto diskette; typing may be no more an art than is fly-fishing, but her work is surely artful in its perfection.

My wife, Marsha Karle, though cheerfully uninterested in learning to fish, is still my best companion on any stream.

My agent and friend Rick Balkin was as always a great help. At Simon & Schuster, Bob Bender, Johanna Li, and Carol Catt were great to work with, and improved the book in many ways. I am delighted to have Eldridge Hardie's splendid drawings accompany my words; I've admired his work for as long as I have fly fished.